MY wonderful JOURNEY through LIFE
with God, Family, and Friends

Rev. Warren C. Biebel, Jr.

MY WONDERFUL JOURNEY THROUGH LIFE
WITH GOD, FAMILY, AND FRIENDS
Copyright © 2016 by Rev. Warren C. Biebel, Jr., and Peak Publishing
Published by:
Peak Publishing • 6700 Wadsworth Blvd., Apt. 101 • Arvada, CO 80003
www.healthylifepress.com

Author: Rev. Warren C. Biebel, Jr.
Designer: Judy Johnson

Printed in the United States of America

No part of this publication may be reproduced, stored in a retrieval system, or transmitted in any form or by any means—for example, electronic, photocopy, recording—without the prior written permission of the author, except for brief quotations in printed reviews.

Library of Congress Cataloging-in-Publication Data
Biebel, Warren C.
My Wonderful Journey Through Life

ISBN 978-1-939267-15-3
1. BIO018000 BIOGRAPHY & AUTOBIOGRAPHY / Religious
2. BIO026000 BIOGRAPHY & AUTOBIOGRAPHY / Personal Memoirs

Unless otherwise noted, Bible quotations are from the King James Version.

This book is available in paperback and hardcover versions. Contact the publisher: info@healthylifepress.com for information about how to obtain the hard cover version.

Most Healthy Life Press resources are available wherever books are sold. Distribution is primarily through www.Amazon.com, www.deepershopping.com, and www.healthylifepress.com. Multiple copy discounts available directly from Healthy Life Press. Wholesale distribution is through www.SpringArbor.com (a division of www.IngramContent.com), and www.deepershopping.com. Our ePublications are available through www.healthylifepress.com, www.Amazon.com (Kindle), www.BN.com (Nook), and for all eBook readers through www.deepershopping.com. Wholesale copies of our eBooks are also available through www.IngramContent.com (www.SpringArbor.com). Combination offers of printed and electronic books of the same title are available at a discount from the publisher at: www.healthylifepress.com. Resources ordered directly from the publisher receive free shipping. For information on our products, or how to publish with us, e-mail: info@healthylifepress.com.

The opinions expressed in this book are those of the author and/or any other contributors and may not represent the official position of Healthy Life Press, its publisher, or any of its other authors.

Dedication

This book is dedicated to my wife, Marian, who has been my faithful companion through thick and thin since we married in 1949, and without whom many of the things described in these pages could not have happened. There are no words that could possibly express my gratitude to the Lord for bringing us together and for allowing us to make this journey together these many years. I love you, dear.

Acknowledgements

A book like this can only be created by a team, and I am so grateful for the help of each and every one. So thank you:

- To Marian, my wife, for converting my hundreds of pages of handwritten scribblings into text that could be edited and then published.
- To Dean Borgman, my lifelong friend, for reading the earlier manuscript and providing a foreword.
- To my father, who so thoughtfully collected, labeled, and preserved so many of our family photos.
- To Judy, my daughter, for investing so many hours in seeking and then providing access to so much family history and family photos.
- To sons Dan and Paul for their contributions and confirmations of details that only they would know.
- To Dave, my other son, for encouraging me in this and my other writing projects, and for helping get them all to print.
- To Judy Johnson, our designer, who made everything look so great!

Thank you, one and all.

Contents

Foreword

Prologue

Learning to Live – My Early Years	1
A World at War and My Personal Peace	11
College Days and Amazing Events	29
God's Call to Begin Things	47
Twenty Great Years of Blessing with a Touch of Sorrow	125
Memories, Memorials, and Many Special Friends	139
New Directions, Opportunities, and Blessings	173
Saving the Best for Last – Back Home in New Hampshire	197
My Personal Photo Album	207

Foreword

WARREN WAS ONE OF MY BOYHOOD FRIENDS—A CLOSE FRIEND. What I remember most about him, as we went through grade school and high school together, was his amazing energy. Back before boyhood became structured by organized Little Leagues, Pop Warner and town soccer teams, Warren was the organizer of our afternoon games. Touch football in the fall, but especially baseball in the spring. He had his eye on a large empty lot, and he sold us on the idea of transforming it into a baseball diamond.

We were Black Rockers. We called Black Rock the 49th state, which is one way of dating us. Black Rock was west of Bridgeport, Connecticut's West End. One day, off Black Rock Yacht Club, we two caught more flatfish in one outing, fifty or something as I remember it, than the number of fish I have caught through the rest of my life.

Reading his candid memoirs, I realize we were both in awe of our cute second grade teacher, Miss Contellini, and later attracted to our pretty and sparkling classmate, Sally Gronberg. More seriously and a few years later, Marian Miller was as attractive, charming and fun as Warren describes his high school sweetheart . . . and his wonderful life partner.

Warren brought his natural enthusiasm and energy into the Christian faith and ministry. Most of us teenagers were coasting along in the Christian life, some of us crazier than others. Warren could have wild fun, but he was a down-to-business Christian leader from early on.

This is an interesting and inspiring book for us ordinary folks—as most of us are. It is about an ordinary person with extraordinary experiences. Warren makes it clear that as a sometimes lonely only child, he was an ordinary child from an ordinary family. It was not a family of strong religious faith—or of great material means. Faith he would find down on the corner of Ellsworth St. and Bartram Ave, at Black Rock Congregational Church. There, Warren would find extended family and spiritual support—sending him off to King's, and then Gordon College . . . and beyond that to Gordon Divinity School.

Warren Biebel was, as he describes himself, just an ordinary guy, but someone, like the ordinary disciples Jesus chose, through whom God would do extraordinary things. The extraordinary things Warren has accomplished in his own family, in individual after individual, in youth program after youth program, in church after church, and yes, in community after community, are all told in an ordinary way to the glory of Jesus Christ and the God he has served.

With many other things pressing, and late into the night, I kept reading this memoir . . . because I love stories . . . of real people, honestly told. Here is the dark as well as the bright, the sad along with happiness, the downs as well as the many ups.

Some of this life I knew, but I was intrigued to be taken into aspects of Warren's life I didn't know, hidden treasures of God's grace and abundant blessing. I have taken kids to Singing Hills and visited it later on. I have called Warren on occasion in Florida . . . and will now call him back in the New Hampshire he loves.

Here is truly an ordinary life with an extraordinary God. You will enjoy this book because it is real as well as very special. It is meant, I believe, to inspire us, more than to celebrate Warren. God's extraordinary through our ordinary is the way of the Gospel. May we all be encouraged to follow our Lord Jesus Christ through thick and thin, knowing that our feeble efforts in sowing the seeds of God's Word will blossom into the kind of fruit Warren Biebel's life has produced.

You are about to read Warren's story: dreamer, builder, servant-leader, admirable family-head, sportsman, helper of many in need . . . and a great friend—always raising the ordinary to extraordinary. To God be the glory.

~ Dean Borgman

Dean Borgman has been for many years a professor at the school Warren Biebel attended (now Gordon-Conwell Theological Seminary), and an Episcopal priest.

Prologue

As I write this book about my life, I am humbled by God's grace as it unfolded over the years. Only He knows why He chose me to be His servant these many years. I surely was not worthy to participate in such a grand adventure. For those of you who pick up these pages to read, if you don't want to be bothered with names and people whom you may not know, I would suggest just to scan it. On the other hand, if you are interested in how God works in a life and family, read it carefully and be aware that my life and ministry has been, and continues to be, about people.

God brought hundreds and maybe even thousands of people into my life, some only briefly, and others for many years. Of all of those, my wife and family are very special. Others became long-term friends and still others just crossed my path and were gone. I want you to see that each one was special to me and my first thought about them was a spiritual question: "Do they know the Lord Jesus?"

You will find that I spent much of my life involved in personal recreation and sports, both for myself and for others. You can rightly ask the question; "Why?" Because of the people! Whether children, teenagers or adults, they are special objects of God's love and sometimes, to meet and fellowship with them in such an environment provided my only opportunity to share my faith in Christ. To be honest, though, there were many times when I desperately needed to restore my mind, body and spirit. Paul wrote to young Timothy in 1 Timothy 4:1-2 and made a connection between physical and spiritual health. He indicated that physical exercise had a place but should always be superseded by spirituality (godliness).

The other ingredient of this story that I hope you notice is that my entire life has been a "connected" experience. Perhaps the most important feature of it all was my immersion in the Bible, a "Lamp" to keep me from stumbling over the stony places and a "searchlight" to give me a vision for the longer difficult road ahead. Yes, there have been sorrows and disappointments, but there has been much more happiness and inspiration.

As time for me in this life dwindles down, I pray that I may serve Him 'til that moment when He says, "come". Oh, that my family and friends will experience the same joy and blessings I have known.
THAT IS MY PRAYER FOR THIS BOOK!

~ Rev. Warren C. Biebel, Jr.

Learning to Live

—⚏—

My Early Years

Baby Warren (that's me) came into the world scene on May 18, 1928. That day would prove to be one of highs and lows for my Mom and Dad, Warren and Mary. I began my life that day and my grandfather, Herman Biebel, had left this life two days earlier, on May 16, 1928! He was a long-time fire fighter, had a heart attack and died that same day.

Mom and Dad were doing great in a fast-changing world. Dad designed cars like the Duesenbergs and others. He worked in New York City on the sixty-third floor of the Chrysler Building to which he commuted daily from Bridgeport, CT. Mom was secretary to the President of the Bridgeport Gas Light Co. Everything was great!

Then, in one day (October 24, 1929) it was all gone! Our little family had nothing —no jobs, no money, and only a small rental flat with no furniture, except beds.

Yes, that's me way back in 1928. And I can still curl my toes like that, too!

Dad took it very hard and fought depression as best he could. It was no fun for him to go from a great job at the Chrysler Building to government bread lines, just to survive. Mom was the strong one and she was the one to help carry us through.

I can't remember much about my first years, but I do remember feeling lonely a lot. I was an only child, and felt jealous of other kids who had brothers and sisters. But that changed with the beginning of my first day at Black Rock School. In those years, in kindergarten through eighth grade, we were taught the importance of faith, honesty, discipline, good health, and patriotism.

The day opened with prayer and the Pledge of Allegiance in the main auditorium. In the classroom, we put our hands on the desk while our teacher checked for dirty fingernails. Miss Contellini, our young, attractive teacher was the future wife of all the 4th, 5th, and 6th grade boys. Black Rock School was a great community place for children. For me it was hard work, but lots of fun while striving to do well. We had art class, various clubs, and I excelled with a drawing of the U.S. Capitol building.

We looked forward to recess outdoors in the big school yard. Dodge ball and tag were popular games. I learned a good lesson from the unfortunate experience of a boy who put his tongue on the metal basketball pole in the freezing weather, and it had to be pried off using hot water. Once a week in the early afternoon,

I was a proud member of our drum corps, which marched in every local and city parade.

we would have a released time period for religious instruction. The Catholic children would walk with a teacher to St. Mary's Church, perhaps a half mile from the school. The Protestant children (including me) would walk about the same distance to Black Rock Congregational Church where we would have a Bible lesson.

Our school was big on singing and instrumental music and we had a Drum Corps which marched proudly in every local and city parade. I played a drum and we dressed proudly in sailors' uniforms. Around and around the block we went until Miss Holroyd, our Principal, was happy with our work. My Grammar School period was a mixture of boredom and excitement.

One of the things I looked forward to in a big way was the visit of my cousins, Paul and Leslie Mitchell. On the certain day they would be coming, I would sit down by Route #1 anxiously looking for their big Packard to arrive from Wethersfield, CT, a rural town near Hartford. Paul, especially, was great at making paper airplanes and soon we had them flying all around the room.

We lived at 55 Haddon Street, an apartment complex. O.J., a character right out of the movies, lived downstairs. He wore a Derby hat, smoked a big cigar, and drank a lot, but I never saw him drunk.

During the summers, Long Island Sound and the beach provided a very happy time for me. An old rowboat, swimming, fishing, collecting crabs and clams, made my days. Not a worry in the world. Our summer home consisted of an old, rickety cottage on a stretch of Long Beach, far from anything. We had to get supplies either by walking over a mile on the sand or by boat. Dad had a twenty-one foot, boat with an inboard motor, which transported supplies up a backwater area called the "crick."

The beach provided endless hours of fun and a wide variety of activities for any kid with a good imagination.

He sold it after a scary incident when he navigated too close to a big freighter and was almost swamped.

Our cottage had no amenities, including no bathroom, and no running water. Instead, all drinking water had to be brought in and a two-seater outhouse provided bathroom facilities. We hosted lots of family members even though sleeping accommodations were sparse. (I often wound up on a very small metal cot or in a tent). Les and Paul Mitchell were interesting cousins. Both later graduated from Yale University and became officers in the U.S. Navy. But when we were kids at the beach, one of Paul's favorite activities was to go along the shore and write, "Foo" in the wet sand. "Foo" was an expression found often in a comic strip of the day. So, along the beach for quite some distance you could often find that word inscribed! I never knew what message it conveyed.

In 1938 the great hurricane hit New England, killing over 500 people and washing away our beloved cottage, except for the soapstone kitchen sink that dropped down and became embedded in the sand. It was another of those really big losses that we experienced, but like the others, there was nothing that could be done about it, so we just carried on.

In those years, the school years were great for me, too. I had several special friends: Dean Borgman, Dick Brown, and my special friend was Ray Alvey. and Bill Koerner was another! Ray's family was a little better off than we were and I often visited their home, on the next street, where Ray and I played with his Ives electric trains, something I have continued to enjoy (model trains) throughout my life. We created all kinds of layouts with the limited tracks and switches we had. One time his family invited me to accompany them on a trip to Canada. We visited a farm where I encountered a huge Tom turkey that chased me down the dirt path. I think of him every Thanksgiving dinner.

Dean's family were devoted Christians with eight children and a nice home for that period. His dad was an executive with the J.L. Lucas Co. They owned a lot behind their home where we played various sports, but especially football, mostly passing and kicking. I remember working really hard to improve that lot, leveling and cutting - perhaps a precursor to my love for landscaping and outdoor work.

Another love of ours was to go down to the Black Rock Yacht Club and fish off the dock. It was easy to bait a multiple hooked drop line with sand worms and pull up two or three flounder (flat fish) at a time. I remember looking out in the harbor and wishing I could get a ride some day on Mr. Borgman's boat, which was moored there. The Borgmans were very devout Christians and had daily devotions. Sometimes, I would be there at the right time and was deeply impressed with the intensity and reality of their faith.

Although my mom and dad were wonderful parents and had a churchgoing past, the Great Depression had disillusioned them and I

The great hurricane of 1938 took away our cottage, another great loss we weathered together.

can't recall them ever taking me to church though they enrolled me in Sunday school and release time from public school.

Dad did do some great things for me, especially taking me on trips to New York City on different occasions to see the ships, the Ice Capades, Ranger hockey, and the Museum of Natural History—and, oh yes, Radio City Music Hall.

Arnold Borgman had a family rule that forbade sports activities on Sundays. Meanwhile, Black Rock had a semi-pro football team and, Dean, my friend, somehow managed to slip away one Sunday to watch a game with me. How could I forget his dad coming and finding him hiding in the crowd and taking him home to be disciplined?

As for me, I had lots of problems growing up, although most of them were from being obnoxious or doing small pranks, stunts, and sometimes things I knew were flat out wrong. One of these involved a Sundry and Cigar store owner. I can't recall his name but he had a huge nose and we (the boys) gave him the name "Moose." We also found that it was easy to help ourselves to small packages of candy or gum in his store, which I knew was very wrong.

As for girls, we were still in the hair-pulling and "making fun" stages. One such girl, Sally Gronberg, was the apple of many a boy's eye and her pigtails made perfect targets for pulling. Seventh and eighth grades came and went with not many changes in behavior, although riding our bikes became a daily activity. I had a new Columbia bike which Dad bought sacrificially for my

My beloved Columbia bike, which I rode everywhere, was a special gift from Dad.

birthday and our favorite ride was to St. Mary's by the Sea, a stone breakwater and road that encompassed a point extending out into Long Island Sound. Dad had finally gotten a job as a meter reader with the Bridgeport Gas Company, which included a car, which we really needed. Yes, it was a step down from designing fancy cars in Manhattan, and it came with some dangers (such as when he had to disconnect somebody's gas for non-payment, and the client got belligerent). But he was faithful with that job until he retired, for which he deserves a great deal of respect.

Christmas was always very special. Even in the poverty years, Mom and Dad made my Christmas a highlight. There was always a beautiful tree, and early on the celebration included Lionel trains with a layout around the tree, complete with switches and gates. How I loved that!

Then the time came to move on! On May 18, 1941, I turned thirteen years old and was in the eighth grade. The war in Europe was expanding, the Nazi blitzkrieg was on in Europe, and the United States was preparing, but not fast enough, to join the battle against the Axis powers. In Europe, nation after nation was falling. My cousins Paul and Leslie were graduating from Yale, and as was customary, they were given commissions in the Navy as Lieutenants, Junior Grade.

As for me, still in the eighth grade, we had daily practice in preparing for attacks. At a signal we would get down under our desks. There were also other kinds of drills like evacuation. Although missiles hadn't been developed then, there was a real fear of bombing and shelling, especially since there were German U-Boats prowling Long Island Sound.

Then December 7, 1941 (when the Japanese fleet attacked Pearl Harbor) changed everything for everybody. Even though the draft had been instituted, men eighteen through thirty and even older were suddenly drafted or volunteered and were gone. Only those who couldn't pass the physical exam were left behind. My cousins, David and Frank, Jr. Munich were called. David had a physical disability and was rejected. Frank, Jr. joined the Army Air Corps. These two were favorite cousins of mine. They both were Boy Scout leaders and were loved by all the boys in Troop 40. As scouts, we were given official badges and taught to be on the lookout for spies along the shores of Long Island Sound (Note: Spies did actually land on eastern Long Island).

Our family had moved from the apartment on Haddon Street to an upstairs rental flat on Morehouse Street. This would prove to be very important to me! Our landlord was a Turkish man who spoke little English. He smoked a long pipe with a bowl that looked like the front of a trumpet. There was a driveway and yard where Dad kept his company car and meticulously cleaned it often.

It was then that Dad gave me that beautiful Columbia bike, which I rode everywhere. Dick Walsh was a neighbor, a little older than me, but we played lots of games of Monopoly, especially during the time when we both had the measles. We also played touch football and other outdoor sports in the street. Across the street from our house was a huge cherry tree. During the fruit season, I would climb that tree to pick and eat as many cherries as I could reach.

One of our neighbors on Morehouse Street was George Barnes, a young man in his late teens. It was George who got a bunch of us younger boys to go to a boys' youth group at Black Rock Congregational Church. The meetings there consisted of rough games like "chicken," which resulted in not a few holes in the wall of the downstairs auditorium. The object of "chicken" was to have one large, strong boy put a smaller, lighter boy on his shoulders and then try to knock the other pairs out of the game. (This wouldn't be allowed today.) After the games we would go to a small room upstairs for "devotions." It was there that Joe Gyana, a soldier home on leave with a war wound, gave a short message from John 3:16.

That night all the childhood sins and wrongs I had done touched my heart even though the message was so simple. Everybody knows John 3:16, right? Not me, at least not before that: "For God so loved the world, that he gave his only begotten Son, that whosoever believeth in him should not perish, but have everlasting life."

I didn't know what, but I knew something very big had happened within me. I felt that all the loneliness, the stealing from the cigar store and other things, as well, had been lifted. I had started a new life! At the time, I was almost fifteen years old.

A World at War and My Personal Peace

I became engrossed in my new life as a Christian, but I did make mistakes. I was especially concerned about Mom and Dad, but took the wrong approach toward them (talking about sin and forgiveness and salvation) and since all my faults and sins were very clear to them, their response was to hope that my new life would go away or at least settle down. But it didn't!

At the same time, my education moved from Black Rock School to Whittier Junior High. Whittier was about five miles from my home on Morehouse Street and necessitated a walk every day to and from school. There were no school buses. The community bully at the time was a boy named Paul McViddy. For some reason he selected me as a target, and I must admit, I didn't like it and kept as far away from him as possible. The interesting sequence to this experience is that this same Paul McViddy would later come back into my life as a Christian and pastor of one of the larger churches in Miami, FL.

The only other thing I remember about Whittier is a speech given in the auditorium by one of the students. It was called, "If you can't trust the United States Government, whom can you trust?"

Then came high school! Bassick High was a large high school for that time. It was located about half-way between my home and downtown Bridgeport, CT. This necessitated those of us living in Black Rock taking a city bus every day to and from school. The cost was 5 cents. The problem for me was getting to the bus stop on Fairfield Avenue on time. If we missed the first bus, the next one, five minutes later, would get us to school just as the bell was ringing to go to class. My room was on the second floor, which required a race up the stairs.

One day, a group of us boys were all late and we agreed to skip the bus and take the day off, better known as playing "hooky." However, as we were standing on the corner deciding what to do, a police cruiser appeared and we all scattered. I ran down the street and into a vacant lot that had high grass. But when I finally returned to the street, there was Sgt. Vin McKelvey, my scout master, who strongly advised me to go home and own up to my parents (which I did).

Sgt. McKelvey was the leader of our scout troop, which met in the Black Rock Police station. Vin was a strong believer in building men in preparation for their war time experiences. One of the things he did was to have boxing matches, using large padded gloves. Being an only child and having had no interaction, physically, like punching or hitting, I was afraid to be chosen for a bout. Maybe that's why I was the first one chosen, and to make it worse, my opponent was Dick Brown, one of my best friends. In the very first minute of the bout, I took a lucky, wild swing and knocked Dick down. I felt really bad about it, but psychologically it went a long way toward curing my fear of the bully, McViddy.

My early days of high school occurred during the worst days of World War II, 1942 through 1944. Because all the able-bodied men had gone to war, including many of the teachers, we were taught by those who came out of retirement, were too old to serve, or elderly women. For the most part they did a good job, but there were a few "bad apples." One of those was our Spanish teacher, Mr. Epstein, who had a foul mouth and made passes at the girls. One day some of the bigger boys in the class put the teacher out of the window on a broad ledge. I personally removed myself from that scene.

Dean Borgman and I had our event, too. In chemistry class, we learned that potassium permanganate in crystal form can produce minor explosions when stepped upon. In a "fun" plan Dean and I stayed in the locker room when the others had gone upstairs to the gym. We scattered the crystals on the floor and then joined the class upstairs. Imagine the excitement we had when little explosions could be heard. But our excitement was cut short when our Principal, Mr. Roth, appeared, coming up the stairs with his purple colored shoes—result—thirty days in detention!

During the time period of 1942-1943 I had two jobs. One was at Landy's drug store at the corner of Fairfield Avenue and Park Avenue in Bridgeport, CT. I was (as it was called in those days) a "soda jerk." This was my first real paying job even though it was only 50 cents an hour, but it did include lots of ice cream, not a bad "perk," I must admit. The other job was for the warm season only, as a caddie at Brooklawn Country Club, a private course for wealthy men. Joe Petrino was our caddy master and made assignments. The going caddy rate at that time was $1.20 for eighteen holes, doubled for carrying two bags. We had a caddie field day at the end of the season with races in the pool and prizes for the winners and then something special, a free round of golf. This was undoubtedly the beginning of my love for the game. I began to play as often as possible at the city course.

About that time, my family, including our dog, "Woofie," moved into my grandmother's house on Ridgefield Avenue in Bridgeport. The occupants included our family of three, Grandma and Grandpa Munich, Great Grandma Brooks, and an Aunt Mabel. Great Grandma Brooks had been married at age sixteen, just after the Civil War, to Roland Brooks, who fought in many battles for the North. He had enlisted when he was fourteen and had fought at Port Hudson, Antietam, and other battles, and for a short time, had been a prisoner of war. So I did have a direct connection with the Civil War, hearing many stories from my Great Grandmother Brooks.

Since I was an only child, I spent a lot of time with my good friend, Woofie.

The days at Ridgefield Avenue were interesting, with lots of big family get-togethers. Playing cards around a huge table was a common activity for the men, including me. An old wind-up Victrola provided the music. But the biggest things for me were access to the telephone and also learning to drive with my Grandma Munich, who took a much more liberal attitude toward my involvement in the activity than my folks did.

One day we were out driving in her green Nash, going all of fifteen miles per hour, when Gram headed straight toward a trolley car and then ran right into it. She was fine, but I got a small bump on the head. The positive outcome of that was her purchase of a large cream-colored Lasalle, and it wasn't long before I was driving that car.

In the meantime, I had been elected President of our teenage group at Black Rock Church and I was calling every teenager I knew, inviting them to come to our Saturday evening meetings. But I was calling someone else, too: Marian!

At "Teenagers" (the church deacons had made a building available for us to use) we had meetings every Saturday night that included a brief message by a guest speaker, lots of rousing singing, games, refreshments, a closing testimony, and prayer time. Teens came from everywhere and one such group (mostly girls) came all the way from Milford, about twenty-five miles away, by bus. With this group of girls was a very pretty one, Marian Miller, who was an immediate attraction to me. In relation to Marian, my efforts to draw attention to myself almost ended in early disaster when, during the game time part of the meeting, Dick Brown and I were playing pitch and catch with a Ping-Pong ball and paddle and I hit a great curve ball that landed perfectly in a cup of cocoa that Marian was just about to drink. Down the front of her clothes went the cocoa, which was bad enough. But I made the mistake of offering her $1.00 to have it cleaned. Her reaction was not too gracious, but it wasn't long before a lifelong relationship began.

Something else also started at that youth group. One Saturday night, I gave my first message, from John 3:16, complete with an invitation. Although no one responded that night, one girl, Dorothy, came up to say that she was 'interested and wanted to know more. I suggested that she take her Bible, read the first chapter of John, then get down beside her bed at home and seek the Lord. That week, I prayed that she might find Him and that she'd be back to tell me the next Saturday.

Well, Saturday came and she was not there, but a friend of hers handed me a letter in which she said she had accepted Christ as Savior—my first soul saved! I was so moved by that, that I went alone into the main church sanctuary, got down on my knees and dedicated my life to the Lord for service. I was deeply serious! As I looked up, there was the huge mural of Jesus holding a lamb in His arms. Two relationships were starting that would last all my life.

Meanwhile, this was the period of 1942 through 1944 (the deepest, darkest time of World War II). Paul and Leslie Mitchell and Frank Munich ("Junie" to us) had gone off to war, Paul and Leslie to the Pacific on battleships and Frank Jr. to England with a squadron of P-51s. They were all in the prime of life. To our sorrow, "Junie" came home, having contracted tuberculosis in England. After a horrific trip home on an oceangoing tugboat in bad weather, he died in the Veterans' Hospital in Rutland Heights, MA. This was a very sad time for Aunt Mazie (Junie's mother) and his brother, David, as well as the entire family. Yet in the face of it, they all managed a spirit that made a huge impression on me. Our family stood together in the loss of our favorite family young man.

You can see from Marian's high school graduation photo why it was love at first sight!

While devoting a lot of my time to "Teenagers" and even more to Marian, I also had several jobs. One was at the Sprague Meter Co. where I worked for one summer and received a pay of 60 cents per hour. In order to work, I had to join a union and pay dues. I did play third base on the company team in the City Industrial League and we were issued uniforms, which probably didn't improve our games. In one game a batted hard ball took a bad bounce and struck my kneecap, an injury that stuck with me permanently.

A little later, I worked at the E.I. Dupont Co. In Fairfield, CT, where I was a "runner." My job was to take messages and tools between departments. Sometimes the older workers would have some fun at the expense of young fellows like me, who were usually pretty naïve about what happened in factories. So, on one of my first days at work, my boss said to me, "I want you to go down to the finishing department and get me a sky hook."

Down the long aisle I went, through every department with their machines churning away and people busily working—a new world to me—in search of a "sky hook."

Imagine my surprise when I finally arrived at the end of the building and asked the mechanics for a sky hook. From their smiles and comments, it only took a second for me to realize the truth that I had been taken! (The "skyhooks" on helicopters today had not yet been invented.)

As I remember it, though, together with the feeling of complete stupidity, there was a certain sense of achievement because when I sheepishly returned to my department, I really belonged to the crew for the first time.

That feeling increased not long thereafter, when my boss sent me off to find a "left-handed monkey wrench." I was young, eager to please, and not mechanically inclined, so I did what I was told, only to see the smiles and hear the laughter of the crew, again.

Dupont was on a war contract making weather gear for the Army. The material was like a heavy plastic and was loaded into huge roller machines that compressed it into sheets. As it came out of the machines, a man would use a hand knife to cut it off to size. One of my friends,

Billy Roberts, a boy a little older than me, had that job and made a big mistake one day. In cutting the material, he cut off a part of a finger with the razor sharp knife.

Great Grandmother Brooks received a widow's pension from the Civil War service of Roland, her late husband. For several years, she made it possible to rent a summer cottage at Lordship Beach for the family. What a great time that was! For me, the boating, swimming, and fishing were great fun. In the evenings some of the other Lordship teens and I would go down to the Crystal Ball Room for a few hours of roller skating. And there was a great hot dog stand there that featured hot dogs with "the works," including mustard, relish, sauerkraut, and best of all, bacon.

Great Grandmother Brooks generously rented a cottage for us at Lordship Beach.

At the other end of Long Beach, from Lordship, was Pleasure Beach Amusement Park. That too, had roller skating, a roller coaster, dodgem cars, and a merry-go-round along with other attractions. Uncle Frank Munich, who was about eighty years old at the time, loved to roller skate and was thought to be nuts by the rest of the family. It was during that summer that Lou and George Godburn, friends of Mom and Dad, visited us at the Lordship cottage. Their only son, Tom was a strong, handsome young man.

Somehow, Tom stepped on a rusty nail and developed blood poisoning, and since the anti-toxin was not available at that time, Tom later died, leaving his parents heartbroken. They continued our family friendship, but it was never quite the same.

Bob and Mary Carroll and Mike, Bob's dad, often came to the cottage. Bob lived in Flushing, NY, and was an engineer on the New York Central Railroad. Mike was blind but managed to do most everything and was always doing calisthenics. He was proud that he could touch the ground with the palms of his hands. Pinochle was the indoor sport and we were all good at it. Playing by the light from a kerosene lamp wasn't all that easy, though!

All this time, I was continuing to work in Black Rock "Teenagers" and was excited at what was happening. The group continued to grow and I kept busy calling other kids to come. Marian was foremost on my mind, too, and I kept the phone lines burning between Bridgeport and her home in Milford, CT. There were others who were very much interested in her, too, and I was determined to do my best to win her.

The war was raging in 1943 and the tide still hadn't turned in our favor. Still in high school at that time, I worked for the U.S. Postal Service during the Christmas vacation. I carried a large leather pouch filled with mostly Christmas cards. None of them said "Happy Holidays" because it wasn't a happy time for many families. It was sad

This photo shows only a part of our Black Rock "Teenagers" group, of which I was president. (Photo courtesy of Dean Borgman)

to see the gold star flags in the windows and doors of families that had lost a loved one to the war. Yet there was a feeling of love and compassion in the air that made Christ's birthday even more meaningful.

Our family continued to celebrate with family gatherings that were especially important in those days. World War II claimed 405,000 dead and 671,000 wounded—some of our best young people. (We should remember that the population of the U.S. in 1940 was only 132,000,000.) One place we gathered often was at the two-story home of Bill and Ruth Metzger and their daughter, Gladys, and with Archie and Tessie Munich and their girls, Shirley and Doris. All the girls were happy and fun to be with. There were upstairs and downstairs apartments and across the street was the biggest, longest building in the world, the General Electric plant, which was going full-blast on a wartime footing. Not many in our family smoked, but when Uncle Bill and Bob Carroll were there the room would be filled with smoke. As I remember it, none of the ladies smoked.

I always loved snow and earlier when we lived on Morehouse St., whenever it snowed, the Flexible Flyer sled went out with me to the nearest snow-covered hill. In some storms, certain streets were actually blocked off for sledding. It was great fun, except for walking back up the hill.

At Bassick High School, both Dean Borgman and I were in the orchestra led by Mr. Banyas. This might have been the worst high school orchestra ever, and it surely frustrated Mr. Banyans to the extent that he once broke his little baton stick over Dean's head. However, we played well enough to cover special occasions.

I did have two teachers who stood out. One of those was my own second cousin, Charles Carr. He was a bachelor, a graduate of Notre Dame, who carried on a prolonged platonic relationship with a principal from another school, a very nice woman. But it lingered too long (years) and she finally broke their engagement. Charles was our biology teacher and in many ways, very good. He handpicked some of us for trips to Greenwich, CT, to work in a preserve area maintained by the Audubon Society. He packed us into his old Oldsmobile and we traveled down the Merritt Parkway to Greenwich. On one occasion, the engine overheated and he got out, opened the hood and put some chewing gum on the small pipe leak, poured some water (that he kept on hand), into the radiator and we were back on our way. In the wooded area where we worked, there was pruning, cutting, and clearing to do. For lunch, he always brought lots of fresh hamburger. I don't know where he got it because meat was rationed at that time, but it was delicious after cooking over an open fire and smothered in ketchup. Charles would come back into my life from time to time, but years later in a very big way.

Mr. Hamm was our physics teacher and I remember only several things about him. One is that he was a very big man and the other is that he taught us that we didn't really need instruments for certain measurements. He used a telephone pole as an example and said that we could decide the height of it within a very small percentage (1 percent) by "estimation."

My visits to Grandma Biebel's weren't a big part of my life, but they were important! Herman, her husband, and my grandfather, had died, and she lived with my dad's sister, Minnie and her husband Uncle Charlie in an upstairs apartment in another part of town. Her son (my dad's brother) Bill, his wife Grace and their three children lived one block away. My first cousins were Billy, Kenny, and Gracie. The unfortunate thing about this part of the family is that it wasn't very close because of a serious difference of opinion between my father and his brother about the war, that at one time had even come to blows. After that, to my knowledge, they never spoke to each other again.

However, I was never involved in that dispute, so I occasionally visited their home where there was a huge pinball machine in the front hallway. Uncle Bill and his sons were fishermen. He had a twenty-two-foot-long boat with a cabin. They took it out to Middleground Lighthouse, about ten miles out in Long Island Sound, and they almost always came back loaded with bluefish and other varieties, which they sold to the local fish markets.

Our time at Ridgefield Avenue is kind of a blur to my memory. Grandpa Munich was always busy repairing some low-income housing homes that he owned on Koosuth Street (not a great neighborhood). He marched proudly in every city parade. After working hard as he always did, he would come home, stretch out on the couch and go to sleep. On one such day, he just didn't wake up.

My relationship with Marian was getting much more serious and we began doing things together. Most of our activities centered on "Teenagers," but we had lots of other fun, too. Savin Rock amusement park, located in Woodmont, near Milford, had lots to do, including all the featured rides. "Dodgems" were electrified cars that you drove, always trying to bump the others. There was a ride that consisted of enclosed seats mounted on long armatures which went around and up and down, and of course a roller coaster, a good test for the stomach.

I was traveling quite often to pick up Marian in the Lasalle and our favorite stop was at a new fast food restaurant named Danny's. It was a precursor to McDonald's and a great place to have a hamburger and other goodies.

A World at War and My Personal Peace

Many events at Black Rock Church affected my life. The pastor had resigned and Harry Cox was the interim pastor. Harry was a gentle, soft-spoken man whose messages were very deep and effective. He and his wife, Cora, had been missionaries in Nigeria where they had established a school and hospital. They also had experienced the loss of their son, who drowned in a well while they were there. This seemed to give their faith an even greater authenticity.

Percy Crawford was an evangelist, well known especially in Philadelphia and the Northeast for his radio ministry "The Young Peoples' Church of the Air." Percy had also founded King's College, located on a former plantation outside Wilmington, DE. It would be at King's that I would begin my college career. The war in Europe was turning in our favor after some very hard-fought battles. My future special friend, Cecil Breton, had to evacuate his B-24 bomber after the plane was hit with anti-aircraft shrapnel and barely made it back to the base. Cecil had to jump out the bomb bay door and in doing so incurred a back injury that would plague him permanently. "Ceece," as we called him, was a wonderful golfer and played at a semi-pro level, always having to deal with the back injury. We became good friends later at Gordon College, leading to a lifelong friendship.

Although things were getting better at home, the war in the Pacific was a different story. However, a miraculous event happened at the Battle of Midway, when our much smaller fleet decisively destroyed a Japanese task force that was far superior in number and fire power. Japanese kamikaze pilots were fa-

Cecil Breton ("Ceece") and I began a life-long friendship during our college days.

natics, not only willing but eager to give their own lives by crashing their bomb-laden planes into our ships. "Kamikaze" was a Japanese word meaning "spirit wind." It was spiritually sacred to these pilots. It was during one of those attacks that my cousin, Paul Mitchell, was stationed in the observation tower of the battleship, Idaho. The Kamikaze planes were coming in below him with huge explosions and fire. The ship survived the attacks, but Paul's hair turned white overnight, a reminder of what naval warfare could do to a person.

During the summer of 1945, a large group of teens from Black Rock spent a lively week at Pinebrook Bible Conference in East Stroudsblurg, PA (Amish country). Although one or two cars made the trip, including Joe Cantor's station wagon, most of us went by train. We started in Bridgeport on the New York, New Haven, and Hartford line, which had electrically powered engines. We transferred in New York at Grand Central Station, to the Delaware, Lackawanna for the trip to Stroudsburg. Being in the late summer, it was very hot on the train and with no air conditioning, the windows had to be kept open. This would have been fine except for the smoke and embers coming in from the coal-fired engine, which emitted black clouds of soot and smoke. The open windows were like a vacuum to pull the soot inside.

We "Black Rockers," as Percy Crawford once labeled us, could be pretty wild sometimes.
(Photo courtesy of Dean Borgman)

The week at Pinebrook was very eventful. Since the war was still on, staff members were hard to get and Percy Crawford, himself, had to do maintenance. That was when the Black Rock group pitched in to make repairs and clean the campus. However, we were also involved in another kind of incident. We (the boys) were very noisy, mostly singing and talking, and we kept it up in our cabins at night. The male staff members lived in cabins not far away; after putting up with our noise for some time, they came up to our area and told us to "shut up." That was a kind of war cry to us, so we barricaded ourselves in the cabins and began singing the "Volga Boatman" song with the "Yo-Ho-Heave-Ho" and pounding on the cabin wall at the end.

The end result was that the camp staffers came up and after a mêlée wrestled us down to the camp duck pond, which was shallow and really muddy on the bottom. All of us, including the staffers ended up in the water. There was plenty of noise, which brought Percy Crawford himself down with a huge flashlight. Being who he was, things immediately settled down and an inventory of all the campers and staff was taken, which revealed that one of our group was missing. The fear was that he had drowned, but after a search of the pond, he was nowhere to be found.

So, when Percy, who had maintained his dignity through it all, told us to get back to our cabins, we (and the staff) went back sheepishly. In our cabin, we were discussing the missing teen when he suddenly came out from under a bunk where he had been hiding all that time. The next morning Percy Crawford had an announcement at breakfast that went something like this, "I want you Black Rockers to know that I really appreciate all you did to help here at camp, but I'm sure you know that last night was a very bad scene. So I have decided that you will need to do breakfast KP (kitchen police) duty for the rest of the week." We all agreed. That meant dishes, pots, and pans and clean-up. The girls were not included.

The morning of August 14, 1945 started out in the usual way—hot and dry. But that day was anything but an ordinary day because it was the day that Japan agreed to surrender. A group of us, expecting something "big" to happen, skipped the morning Bible session and piled into Joe Cantor's station wagon to go into Stroudsburg. It was during the thirty mile trip that we heard on the radio the good news of surrender. The war was over; the troops would be coming home. The actual formal ceremony took place on the battleship Missouri on September 2, 1945. We came back into camp yelling and blaring the horn, but no one seemed to mind. Everyone was celebrating.

My cousin, Paul, was just outside Tokyo harbor that day on the "Idaho" and sent a letter, which I have, describing the scene and postmarked from the ship that day. He mentioned that the Japanese citizens visible from the ship were paying no attention to the massive fleet in Tokyo harbor.

My cousin, Paul, was in the observation tower during the kamikazee bombing of the battleship, Idaho.

With the ending of the war, many changes took place. For one thing, the military draft ended on my birthday, May 18, 1946, and even though there were other wars to come during my lifetime, I never was in the military.

Troop ships from all over the world, loaded with troops, were arriving daily and disembarking. There were parades and the Navy had ships in New York harbor, open for the public to visit. Marian and I headed to New York along with other friends and soon we found ourselves compressed, like sardines, on subways where the last riders had to be pushed into the squeeze. What a time that was!

The aftermath of the war was a different story. The men were coming home, many after four years of separation from marriages that in many cases had been arranged at the last minute before embarking. Many had been wounded, lost limbs, or had bad memories that were hard to overcome. The government was deeply concerned about the marriage failures and erected many billboards with the advice: "The family that prays together, stays together."

Even though the war was officially over, rationing continued for some time. The nation was adapting to the change, but housing for families and jobs were hard to get. Imagine more than two million servicemen and women, now civilians, trying to enter the work force when defense plants all over the country were shutting down.

President Roosevelt had died and Harry Truman was president. Truman had authorized the atomic bombs that were dropped on Hiroshima and Nagasaki, bringing the quick end to the war with Japan. As the war ended, thousands of allied troops were released from prison camps. There was a marked difference between those who had been prisoners in Europe and those who were imprisoned in Japan. The Japanese had provided only a very meager diet in the Philippines, and many prisoners had died from malnutrition and mistreatment.

Those who survived needed significant healing in bodies, minds, and hearts, but there was some good to be found, overall. Finally, the war was over and now as a nation we could strive to build toward a brighter future instead of focusing on the awful darkness of the recent past.

College Days and Amazing Events

MARIAN AND I HAD A CONTINUING AND DEEPENING RELATIONSHIP. She enrolled in nursing school at Bridgeport Hospital and I headed for King's College, located outside of Wilmington, DE. Marian began a lifelong interest in knitting, beginning with a beautiful green winter sweater, complete with reindeer—that was for me! Our relationship centered in our faith in Christ and I headed to college, envisioning myself as a missionary or minister. While I was at King's, I called Marian and made the trip home as often as I could. I'm sure she loved me, because I was probably one of the worst letter writers, ever.

Things at King's didn't get off to a very good start. I was assigned a room on the third floor of a building that most likely had been the servants' quarters in its plantation days.

While I attended King's College, Marian enrolled in nursing school at Bridgeport Hospital

The room needed lots of work, including painting. It had ten-foot-high ceilings and was a far cry from college dorms today. The beds were army surplus cots and there was an additional small side room, already claimed by Jim Capola, recently discharged from the Army Air Corps.

In addition to Jim and me, our "apartment" housed two other roommates from Black Rock Church—Dick Brown and Jack Kershaw. We had one other roommate—a farm boy named Dave (I don't remember his last name). Dick had been in the Marines, Jack was an older married man, and Dave wore big boots that we called "clod hoppers." This became a story in itself. We had one small bathroom with a shower that had hot water only when the upperclassmen in the lower two wings were not using theirs. In addition, the bathroom was not soundproofed and odd noises often emanated from it. Perhaps the most memorable of those were due to Jack's propensity for lengthy, loud gargling. He had a "thing" for cleanliness. It was tough for Jack, being an older man, to live with us. It didn't take me long to get sick from the smallpox immunization that I'd had before leaving home. I had a fever and lay there thinking that my college career was over.

Then came the "hazing." When we met an upperclassman, we had to take off a "beanie" that was part of the hazing and say, "Hail Ye Nifty Class of 50." As part of my college initiation, one night I was taken out for a "ride," supposedly to get a sub sandwich. Instead, I unwillingly disembarked on a dark country road at their invitation and watched as the car lights faded into the distance. I had no idea where I was and as I surveyed the scene, I could see only one small light in the distance. I don't remember being afraid, but more determined to get back to my dorm. Finally a car came down the road and the driver stopped and offered me a ride and I was quick to accept the offer, but on the short drive to the campus I had my first experience with a "gay." I was completely naïve about this at the time, but I quickly realized when he slowly put his hand on my knee that it was time to get out. "Stop the car," I said. "Thanks for the ride, but no thanks." We were almost to the dorm and after a short walk I was there. It gave me a lot to think about, though.

College Days and Amazing Events

Dave, the farm boy, had a habit of coming in late and the noise of those boots coming up the stairs sounded like artillery. Lots of times we all had dozed off before he came in. It seemed to me that this was where the term "rude awakening" came from. At any rate, we had a "war council" and decided to fix Dave. On a certain night we arranged a bucket of water over the door in such a way that opening the door would trip the bucket and the water would come down on Dave. Imagine our anticipation when we heard those footsteps coming up the stairs. After a momentary pause, the door opened, water came down and there stood . . . not Dave, but the college Dean, Bob Davies. Surprisingly, Bob didn't get mad and no punishment was meted out. He taught us a lesson in grace and good sportsmanship when he simply said, "Come on boys, it's time for bed."

For a Dean of Students, Bob Davies was a regular guy. In addition to his duties of administration, he was the basketball coach. King's had an excellent basketball team for a small college. Many of the sophomore students were service veterans and a bit older than me. I remember admiring them as deep and committed Christians. Some of them wanted to return to minister to their defeated enemies as missionaries. One member of the team was Roy McDaniels. Roy had left the service and as I remember, it was his plan to go back to post-war Japan as a missionary.

These fellows were very athletic and provided coach Davies with an unusually good crop of players. I should have known, after an appraisal of my height of 5 foot 10 inches and lack of experience, that I would warm the bench, but I was determined to try and I did make the team. I was a good ball handler. One of our team players was George Dempsey, who later became a regular in the NBA, playing for the Philadelphia Warriors. As for me, I'll come back to my own basketball "career" later.

The highlight of my time at King's was a very unusual experience, especially in the time frame of our nation's history. Every Friday night, the college would send a bus into the city of Wilmington, DE. Those who wanted to could go into the downtown area and find someone to talk with and share the gospel. On one particular Friday, I was walking around a neighborhood that was new to me. Actually, I knew nothing about Wilmington. I came to a street corner where five young African-American boys were just standing around. Approaching, I asked if they would like to hear a Bible story and they responded with an enthusiastic, "Yes." Thus began an unbelievable sequence of events. At the end of my story, I asked the boys if they would like to meet again and once more the answer was affirmative. I suggested that I would try to find a place to meet and they agreed to be there the following Friday. So, where would I go to find a meeting room? The YMCA, of course. As I came to the desk of the beautiful "Y," I asked the desk man if I might have a room for the meeting. At first he said, yes, but when I mentioned that the boys were African-Americans, he immediately said, "I'm sorry but that isn't possible. They have their own YMCA." And he told me where it was.

Remember, this was 1947 and the city was completely segregated! I did visit the other "Y," where I met Mr. George W. Taylor, a handsome, college-educated black man who received me graciously. After telling him of my idea, I received his enthusiastic approval and we could begin in the gym. There I wound up on Friday nights with not five but fifty or more boys. Those Friday nights were going great and along with the gospel message, the boys had fun with games and sports. Then, Mr. Taylor told me of another place in a low-income housing development, which also had a gym. He would introduce me to the people there, which he did, and as a result, I wound up a sort of "missionary" to two groups of African-American men and boys, and I was the only white.

As we were nearing the end of the season, I got the idea of having a big field day and picnic at our college campus. I approached Percy Crawford with the idea and he immediately answered, "Yes, let's do it." The college would send two buses to bring the "Y" groups out to our

College Days and Amazing Events

campus, which was about twenty-five miles outside of Wilmington, and we would provide hot dogs and marshmallows. Most, if not all, of the boys had never been outside their own neighborhood, let alone, the city, and they were very excited about the idea.

However, something happened that morning that almost canceled the whole plan. Two boys drowned in the "Y" pool. Talking with Mr. Taylor on the phone, we finally agreed together that it would be best to go ahead with the field day. So, the buses arrived with almost a hundred boys and leaders and it was on with the games and later, the food.

Some of my classmates had made a huge pile of wood in the center of the field and as it began to get dark, we had the campfire. I'll never forget how the boys formed a huge circle around the embers of the fire, as I gave a gospel message. As I gave an invitation to receive Christ as Savior, I believe all one hundred raised their hands. Thank you, Lord!

As a good conclusion to a great experience, I arranged for our all-white basketball team to play their all-black team at their gym and it went very well. I believe that this might have been one of the first such events in Delaware, if not in the nation! On my last visit to that "Y" before heading home to Bridgeport, Mr. Taylor presented me with a certificate of appreciation which I treasure greatly.

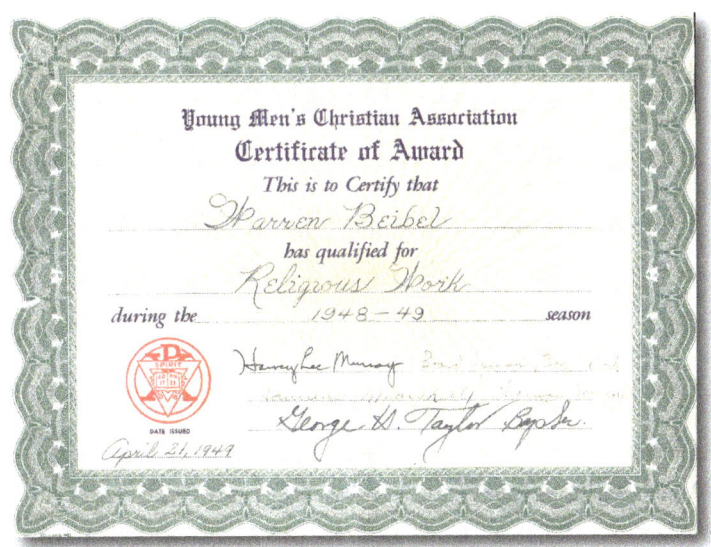

In one chapel service, Percy Crawford tried to enlist volunteers to build a tennis court on campus. The ground near the administration building had been tested and found to be clay. So, the college would provide the hardware if someone would do the work of weeding, leveling, and laying out the court. Guess who volunteered? That would be me and one other student. Well, as a reward, I did get to play a game of tennis with the president of the college, Percy Crawford.

During my second year at King's, I had decided to transfer to Gordon College, in Boston, and my credits had been accepted. But there was still an event that happened on the night before I would be heading home for Christmas vacation and then to return for one final semester at King's. I was still on the basketball team and we had a game with Philadelphia Textile. The game was in Philadelphia and my plan was to take a train after the game, back to Bridgeport. As I recall, we lost the game, but I got to play toward the end and scored two points.

My train left the station around midnight. The car was crowded with people, mostly service men, but I found a double seat where I could lie down. My main concern was that if I fell asleep I might miss my stop. When the train stopped in Norwalk, CT, I sleepily looked out the window, the shade being down half-way. On the platform, outside, was a man holding a woman up. It looked like she was sick or had fainted. However, the man suddenly dropped her into a snow bank and headed for our car. He rushed in the door, cursing, and headed right for me. I was struggling to get up when he, while continuing his harangue, punched me in the nose, breaking it, and also slapped me hard on both

College Days and Amazing Events 35

sides of my face, injuring the joints. Then he left.

I got up to go to the restroom because my face was covered with blood and so was the reindeer sweater that Marian had knitted for me. I saw a conductor and asked him to find out about the man, but he said the train was pulling out.

By the time we arrived in Bridgeport, it was about 3 a.m. My dad was there to take me home, but when he saw me and heard what had happened, he said, "We've got to find the railroad police." Down the stairs we went where we did encounter a railroad security officer. He immediately said, "We've got to stop that train!" So, it was back down the stairs, under the platform and up the stairs, to get us to the train just as it was pulling out. The officer jumped on the car, pulled the emergency cord and stopped the train. He was able to find just two witnesses to my attack, even though everyone had seen and heard it.

The next day, I was excited to see Marian. She was beautiful, but what a sight I was! My nose and face were swollen and all colors of black and green. I had two black eyes. I was scheduled to speak at Black Rock "teenagers" that Saturday night and was determined to do it. Even with my injuries, I still had a wonderful Christmas. That was the winter of 1948. I finished my last semester at King's, attending the graduation ceremonies where Billy Graham was the speaker. Then I packed up my belongings and left for a whole new and exciting chapter in my life.

Things were moving fast in 1949, including the move from Delaware to Boston, starting my studies at Gordon, and finding housing and work. But the biggest and most important event of all happened on March 31, when Marian and I started an adventure together, one that has lasted sixty-six years as I write this. We were married in Marian's own home by Rev. Francis Phillips, pastor of Grace Baptist Church in Milford and our best man was Dick Brown. Marian's sister, Catherine, was bridesmaid.

Marian and I were married on March 31, 1949, in Marian's home, by Rev. Francis Phillips.

Then it was on to Boston, where we shared a house with another family in a neighborhood that was notorious for its mixture of races and radicals, notorious for crime, and one block from Dudley Street station. The house was the parsonage for a small Norwegian congregation and right next to the church. We had to make every dollar count, so every Saturday night we went down to Haymarket Square in Boston to get all kinds of vegetables and bread at very little cost. It was, a "bring your own bag" arrangement. Our diet included lots of potatoes and potato soup doctored up with seasonings. I was working at Gordon, doing maintenance. One of the biggest jobs was helping to move Gordon Divinity School from its original location in Cambridge to Princemere, a large campus about thirty miles north of Boston. Along with other students, we rode in the back of an open truck on top of all kinds of furnishings. We sang some pretty wild songs during the ride. At Princemere, we unloaded at a huge stone building. Mr. Prince, owner of the Prince Spaghetti Company, had donated the building which was made of huge stonework brought from Italy. Unloading and placing the furnishings in their designated spots was no small task. The building consisted of many narrow hallways and small rooms making it hard to make the corners with the large pieces.

Gordon College was located at 30 Evans Way, only a short walk from Fenway Park in Boston. I immediately became a Red Sox fan and since

bleacher tickets were only fifty cents, I got to see more than a few games. On one such occasion, I attended a double-header. In those days, the second game followed the first with a short break in between. So for fifty cents, I got to see Cleveland and Boston fight it out for eight hours. Many Hall of Famers, including Ted Williams, Dom DiMaggio, and Gene Stephens played that day.

Our first child, David Bruce Biebel, was born on August 13, 1949, but he was very premature and had undeveloped lungs, a condition called the "blue baby" syndrome. He was born in Boston Lying-In Hospital (which is now Brigham and Women's Hospital). David was immediately placed in an incubator where he stayed for six weeks. He weighed just over four pounds when he was born, three pounds eleven ounces after his first week. Marian was placed in a ward with other women who had lost their babies. It was an unhappy place, but I tried my best to cheer her up. With our baby barely hanging on to life, I went on with my work as best I could, often calling the hospital to check on his condition. After almost two months had passed, I went to a small room in the church and got down on my knees. I asked the Lord to lay his healing hand on David and stayed there for some time until I had a special feeling that the Lord had answered. I went down to the corner drug store (we didn't have a phone) and called the hospital. What a day that was, when the answer was that he was doing

We finally brought David home after he spent his first six weeks in the Intensive Care nursery.

much better! He had been in the Intensive Care nursery for more than forty days. We were able to hold him for the first time.

At Gordon I was studying and working. I had excellent teachers, including one who stands out in my mind. Dr. Hudson Armerding had been an officer in the Navy (a Lieutenant Commander, I believe) and had been at the battle of Midway. Dr. Armerding believed that God had intervened in that battle to save our fleet. In the famous incident portrayed in the war movies, a Japanese scout plane sighted our ships but could not alert his own much larger, more powerful fleet of our task force's position due to a faulty radio. As history shows, we won a stunning victory in that battle and it was the turning point in our war with Japan. It was a special privilege to hear the story from an eye witness. Dr. Armerding went on to become President of Wheaton College. I remember him most for his soft-spoken, kind character.

I was really sad when Grandma Grace Munich died in 1950.

While there was joy for us in David's improvement and recovery, there was sorrow, too. On March 11, 1950, my grandmother Grace Munich died at Bridgeport Hospital after a long battle with stomach cancer. She was seventy-three years old and had done so much for me. I was really very sad that she was gone. The parties, the old

Victrola, the card games, and the wonderful dinners featuring her roast beef, mashed potatoes, and gravy all were gone but not the memories. I remember, too, that it was Grandma Munich who took me to church with her at St. Paul's Episcopal in downtown Bridgeport.

In the meantime, my parents had been able to purchase a nice little home, located at 235 Raven Terrace in Stratford, CT, not far from Sikorsky manufacturing, the prime supplier of helicopters for the military. They had taken great grandmother, Sarah Brooks, to live with them. The house was rather small, but suited them well and had an upstairs room which we used when visiting.

I don't remember the circumstances that brought it about, but I had an opportunity to caddy in a special tournament at Mill River Country Club, just a short drive from Dad's house. I was assigned to carry the bag for a prominent dentist, and an excellent player. His game was going very well until the eighth green which was near the club house. He was standing on the green, waiting for his turn to putt when a ball came from somewhere and hit him on the head. I'll never forget how the ball hit and went straight up in the air, about twenty-five feet. The poor doctor staggered around and was laid down on the green by his partners and then taken into the club house. He did remember me, though, with a five dollar tip—that was a lot in those days!

My last direct connection with the Civil War ended that summer when Great Grandma Brooks died. Mom and Dad Biebel had gone on a much deserved vacation to Cape Cod and Marian and I were staying at their house taking care of Great Grandma. Suddenly, one night, we heard a strange gurgling sound in her bedroom. It was obvious to me that she was dying, so I took her in my arms and she passed away right there. Born in 1858 and married at age sixteen, she had made possible many wonderful times at the cottages in Lordship. I can't remember her ever being sick before she died at age ninety-three.

———ɯ———

After that summer, we headed back to Boston in our Plymouth, which we had purchased from a Christian dealer in Stroudsburg, PA. It was one of the first new models to come out after the war; it turned out to be a real "clunker." I doubt that any car ever rattled more than that one. Back in Boston, we moved into a one-room apartment with a shared kitchen, which also had a small nook that became a room for David. My experience with trying to wallpaper that room with its nooks and crannies proved to be a total disaster and indicated that it was not my "calling" to do papering. The house itself backed up to Franklin Park, a popular hiking and picnicking place that also had a zoo. Hagop Yaksezian and his wife owned the house. They were immigrants from Lebanon. He provided us with some laughter when we came home one evening and we could see him clearly in his apartment window, removing his toupée!

My Great-Grandfather Roland Brooks fought at Antietam, Gettysburg, and in other battles of the Civil War.

———ɯ———

This was also a time when we were developing a life-long friendship with "Bret" (Cecil Breton) and his wife "Flo." They visited our apartment and we visited theirs, where they were living with Flo's parents. Flo's dad always called David "hot dog" because they would keep him on Sunday nights while we went to Park Street church together with Bret and Flo. They would always feed him hot dogs and he was very happy with that. Bret was also a student at Gordon College and was called to be the pastor of the Natick Chapel. He asked me to be the youth leader. Bret and I were always trading friendly kidding and one night while we were painting the church auditorium, a Scottish man, a member of the church overheard us. Although nothing objectionable had been said, he was deeply offended and it necessitated an apology by Bret. But, what could they expect from Bret's weekly pay of $5.00 and mine of $1.00? The trip to and from Natick did open my life for the first time to an exciting experience—pizza!

I was continuing my maintenance work at Gordon when I was offered, unexpectedly, a coaching job at Dexter School in Brookline. This was a private school for boys. Dexter was a prep school for Harvard and almost all of the boys were children of the wealthiest families in Boston. They recruited part-time coaches from Gordon College because they knew that it was a Christian college. Mr. Davies was the head coach and I was to coach the second grade boy's football team. I had to laugh at these little guys running onto the field in full uniforms, including shoulder pads and helmets. One of my boys was Billy C and another was Richard E. This led to a surprising chapter in my life.

That was the school year of 1950. It was also the year that Billy Graham held a huge rally on Boston Common with 50,000 people in attendance. The weather forecast called for rain, but the day turned out to be fine after many Christians prayed for good weather. Many people turned to Christ at the invitation.

Billy C was the grandson of Mrs. P, who was the owner of a large distributor of premium canned foods. She was very wealthy. After I had coached Billy for a while, I received an invitation to visit Mrs. P's brownstone home which was located on Beacon Hill, just a few doors from the Massachusetts Capitol building. When I arrived, she was very gracious and explained that she would like me to spend the summer tutoring her grandchildren, Billy and Joanne C. This would mean for me to go down to Cape Cod to Oyster Harbors Island and stay there from Monday to Friday. I really needed the work and after conferring with Marian, it was decided that I should take the job.

One of the questions asked by Mrs. P was whether I could teach Billy to sail. I told her honestly about my days of boating on Long Island Sound, but that I had never done any sailing. Even so, I thought I could handle it. I went out and bought a book entitled, *How to Sail*, which described all the parts of a medium-sized sailboat along with terms like "jibing." Also, I would be teaching Billy football. Billy was the nephew of a famous movie star of that period.

Joanne C was about eleven years old. She was having trouble in school particularly with math and English. During the whole summer I never saw either of her parents. I was to tutor her about two hours each morning. Marian accompanied me to Oyster Harbors Island, a private enclave of some of the world's wealthiest. A causeway led out to the island with a guardhouse and guard at the gate. It was necessary to show identification in order to gain entrance. Once on the island, we passed the immense clubhouse with its mile-long sandy beach and fifteen tennis courts. Although I never did see a golf course, I'm sure there was one there.

Mrs. P's summer residence was a twenty-one room house (they called these homes "cottages"). It was situated at the top of a hill with a long stairway leading down to the shore and a river that separated the island from the sand dunes along the ocean side. Part way out an eighteen-foot sailboat was moored. This size sailboat was called "junior class," for races that were held periodically.

Mrs. P suggested that I take the boat out. So down the long stairway I went, into the small skiff and out to the sailboat, fortified by my study of the book, *How to Sail*. It only took a couple of minutes to hoist the sail, after untying the buoy. Wow! The boat and I took off like a shot in the fifteen-mile-per-hour wind. Now what? The river was really a salt water river that connected at each end with Narragansett Sound. It was about one hundred yards across and rose and fell with the tides. There were times when it was filled with fish, especially bluefish.

For me at that moment, the challenge was to turn the boat around before we (the boat and I) hit the shore on the opposite side. The word "jibe" flashed into my mind, I grabbed the rudder handle and the boat suddenly swung around, the boom almost hitting me. It was time to get back to the mooring. So, I was faced with the prospect of getting back to the buoy, taking the sail down, and stopping the forward momentum. I noticed a long wooden boat hook in the bottom of the boat and grabbed it, let the sail down and prepared to grasp the buoy with the boat hook. I did get it on the first pass but was almost pulled overboard when the boat refused to stop quickly. What a comic scenario for Mrs. P and Marian who were standing above, at the top of the stairs, watching the whole thing! Despite that rough beginning, by the end of the summer, I became a pretty good sailor, sometimes taking the boat out in the Sound, even in windy, rough weather.

The stay with Mrs. P was an interesting interlude in my life. She was about seventy years old and she and her African-American maid, Dora, were the only two weekday residents, except for me and the two children. Weekends, though, were totally different, when numerous younger people descended on the property to hold wild parties. Life for all of us was pretty routine, including mealtimes. Tutoring and sometimes outdoor activities occupied the mornings. It was very important, in Mrs. P's thinking, that Billy and Joann's day be completely planned well in advance, including their playmates.

One of those was a granddaughter of the D's, another extremely wealthy family, who came one day to play with Joanne. They decided to explore the attic. I was in my room, studying, when I heard the girls screaming. I hurried through the open panel into the attic and found the visiting girl had caught her foot in the rafters. It was a simple matter to turn her foot and get her out. The result for me was an invitation and subsequent ride on their family's yacht.

It became obvious soon after I arrived that it was really Dora, the cook, who was running the house. Socially, it was vital among the wealthy, elite that they entertain each other and one priority was to have a cook and a maid. Dora did very little work, except on those special occasions. She was always threatening to quit or was laid up with a headache. She did prepare the evening meal which more often than not was "roast duck." Part of the social activities for the older women was to schedule a séance with phony "spiritualists" who plied that part of the Cape, charging exorbitant prices for their services. On evenings when Mrs. P was at home, I often was invited to join her in the living room. I shared my faith in Christ and I questioned the value of her continuing to seek spirituality with these fakes. She seemed gracious in hearing me but I had no outward indication that she responded, although I detected a small hint later back in Boston.

There was another amazing experience in store for me. One foggy, but warm day, Mrs. P asked me to take the children to the beach near the clubhouse. When we arrived there was not a soul there. Billy and Joanne went some distance down the beach where I could still see them. I was lying there on the beach when suddenly I heard beautiful music. Where was it coming from? Turning my head, I noticed a small building where a five piece band was playing great music. This didn't make too much sense, since I was the only one on the beach and I was almost broke financially. Pretty soon the leader approached me and said, "Sir, can we play some of your favorites?" In a confused manner, I said, "No, you're doing great." And that was it, a concert just for me. The explana-

College Days and Amazing Events   45

tion was that the group had a contract to play every morning at a certain time. Usually the beach would be crowded. We were approaching the end of the summer and Mrs. P asked if I would be interested in helping her at her Boston home on Saturdays and offered a fair payment for my work.

How good it was to be back at home with Marian, never to be parted like that again. It may have been by Mrs. P's recommendation that I also had a weekly meeting with five boys from Dexter School. Among the five were Billy C and Richard E. We met in the Unitarian church at the bottom of Beacon Hill. There I would have a short devotional which I am sure would have made some of the Unitarians turn over in their graves. After the devotions, I would take the boys to Franklin Park where they would play games including "hide and seek." Imagine boys from Boston's wealthiest families hiding in the woods at the park. Even then it wasn't the safest of places. Richard E was the son of the president of one of the world's largest insurance companies. He was a middle-aged man with a younger wife and a young son. He approached me

The beautiful stone building on the Princemere estate was renamed "Frost Hall" in honor of Martha Frost.

about coming up to his penthouse in the company's building to play with Richard and his electric trains—this was right down my alley! And to be paid for it! I don't remember too much about that except that on one of my last visits, Mr. E offered his "cottage" on Cape Cod to Marian and me for the fall season. It would be available with all the amenities including several servants who were always there, plus the use of a "Chris Craft" speed boat. I had to turn down his offer as I would be starting my first semester at Gordon Divinity School in September.

God's Call to Begin Things

The year was 1951, and my first semester at Gordon Divinity School included courses in Greek, Ancient Church history, Introduction to the Pentateuch, and Baptist Polity. Although I did study, something else was going on inside me that I couldn't ignore. I had a growing desire and urgency to get going with my ministry so I enlisted in the outreach ministry, a program to supply churches that needed speakers to fill their pulpits. My first opportunity was to speak at a fairly sizeable Congregational church in the Boston suburbs. This was a onetime opportunity, but it did raise an important question—could I in good faith baptize infants? I had two especially outstanding professors, Dr. Roger Nicole and Professor Charles Schauffele (both of whom my son, Dave, had as professors years later when he attended the same seminary). In regard to the baptism question, I sought the advice of Dr. Nicole. Although he himself was of a Reformed persuasion, he gave me advice that changed my uncommitted course and put me on a lifelong path. His advice was, "Study the Scriptures and make your decision on what you find." As a result, I became a Baptist!

My next opportunity to preach was at a small church in North Weare, NH. Arrangements had been made for me to spend the night at the home of Rev. Paul Scruton in the nearby town of Contoocook,

NH. As I drove toward Contoocook, I passed the small white church where I would be preaching the next day and just a short distance down the road, I passed a sign which read No. Weare ("nowhere"). Is that where I would spend my career?

While at Rev. Scruton's, we were having a good conversation when his phone rang. It was someone from the "Youth for Christ" group in Claremont, NH, that met every Saturday night. They were in a bind because their scheduled speaker for that evening had canceled and they were hoping to have Pastor Scruton step in at the last minute. Since he had previously been there several times, he suggested, "There is a young man here from Gordon Divinity School who could fill in." They accepted the offer and so did I!

It was in the early spring and not having been in New Hampshire before, I was not familiar with the meaning of certain road signs. One such sign read, "Frost Heaves"! Unfortunately, I didn't pay any attention and very soon after, I had a bump on my head from hitting the roof. In the late winter and early spring in that part of New England, the roads, which had been frozen during the wintertime, were becoming frost-free, but Jack Frost did not release his grip on those roads all at once, so portions of the asphalt might rise up dramatically or dip down as dramatically from the freezing and unfreezing that was going on day-by-day. I certainly took it slower the next time I saw that sign!

CLAREMONT

I arrived in Claremont, NH, to find the meeting taking place in a hall on the second floor of a building called "The Odd Fellows Hall." Upon entering the large room, I was amazed to find a loosely organized, but very enthusiastic group of almost a hundred people. There was some energetic singing and then it was time for me to speak. My message was the same one I had prepared for the next morning and as I spoke, a toddler came up and followed me around the pulpit that was actually a music stand. But the important thing for me was at the end, one lady named Barbara came forward to receive Christ as her Savior. I didn't know it at the time, but the group was about to try organizing a church and considered the speakers as pastoral candidates. This was mentioned to me before I left and that was "it" for my first visit. I was really impressed with the spirit in that meeting.

Back at our apartment I was continuing my studies but wondering if I would hear any more from the folks in Claremont. In my spare time, I had a small train layout in the attic above our apartment. It was there, too, that I had some deep spiritual times with the Lord and His Word. As the semester was coming to an end and summer would mean finding another job and I was feeling a growing urgency about the ministry. I hadn't heard from the Claremont group. This resulted in my doing something that I would do only a few times in my ministry. I went to the attic, got down on my knees and made a specific request to the Lord. I asked Him to, "Please show me what you want me to do."

Little did I know it but the answer was already in the mail. The next day I received a letter from Mr. Harry Kent, stating that the Youth for Christ group had voted to become a church and had voted unanimously to call me as pastor. A hat had been passed among the group to see how much support could be raised. It was done by anonymous pledge and the amount totaled $41.00 a week. So, I was offered that amount, plus room and board with a farm family, to become their pastor. I discussed this offer with the "outreach" professor and my classmates, because, even in 1951 $41.00 a week was a pretty meager wage with which to support my family. It was the opinion of the Outreach Director that the group probably wasn't going anywhere. However, deep in my heart I knew that the Lord wanted me to go! While all this was going on, the Lord and Marian added another member to the Biebel family, when Dan Martin

Biebel was born in Boston Lying-In Hospital on February 7, 1952.

So, with the Lord leading the way, as He always did, and our little family loaded into our car, with our meager possessions, we headed to New Hampshire. Thus began a wonderful adventure that lasted for forty blessing-filled years. When we arrived in Claremont, we would be living temporarily with the Raymond Mark family who had a large brick farm house in Cornish, NH, a small village just outside Claremont. The Marks had seven children, the older ones pitching in to help their small dairy farm function. The welcome that we received from this family was overwhelming and got me off to a great start. Behind their home was a rock strewn pasture on a steep hill. I had read how Billy Graham, while preparing for his great crusades, practiced preaching on a hillside near the family home in North Carolina. Of course, every young aspiring minister wanted to emulate Billy, so I wound up practicing my preaching among the rocks on that Cornish hillside.

One day, as I was doing that I heard screaming and saw one of the Mark's younger girls, Nancy, floundering in their farm pond. Running down, I pulled her to dry ground. It was an incident I remember well although she may not. Mrs. Mark was great at putting together meals for their family of nine, plus our four, although Dan was still an infant. Most of the food was homegrown, including beef and chicken, plus the milk.

The genius of the gospel was really for one believer to pass the message on to another person and that can be best illustrated by an experience I had in Claremont. Someone told me about a family that needed help and I clearly remember my first visit to the Lamontagne family—Leonard and Esther and their children. Their home was a huge house at the very top of Moody Hill. At one time, it had been a mansion but now was showing signs of deterioration. Coming up the driveway I noticed a number of cars in various stages of disrepair and it was evident to me that Len was an auto mechanic and attempting a home business. My first visit assured me that these were nice people. Len was typical of French Canadian men, a little on the rough and ready side and an avid hunter. He loved to share his hunting stories and it was he that told me that deer could jump backwards, a fact that I discovered to be true in my own hunting experience some time later. But at the time I had a hard time believing it. I was able to initiate a conversation and later a relationship that lasted over the next few years and Esther became a faithful friend at Calvary Baptist. She and Marian had many friendly coffee hours together.

Our children were very compatible with theirs so they spent many afternoons together. But one of the most significant things Esther did was to tell me about a really needy family, Albert, Edna, and Sandy Otten. As a result, I went to visit them at their small upstairs apartment on Maple Avenue, I found that both Al and Edna were sick and the family was destitute. Al had been a hero in World War II in that he had rescued some wounded buddies and dragged them from a frozen river to safety while under fire. For this and other service experiences he had received numerous medals. But, when he returned to Long Island from overseas, life didn't get brighter as he had hoped and he moved his little family to Claremont, NH. I knew immediately that it would take a special blessing from the Lord to save this family. That blessing did come, but it was not without its peaks and val-

Al and Edna Otten became long-time friends and supporters of Singing Hills.

leys in the forthcoming years. Al had found a job driving and delivering bread for Goddard Bakery.

One Christmas eve, Al didn't come home and because he still was battling with mental wounds left from the war, I was afraid of what he might have done. Where was he? And what would we find? I enlisted the help of "Pop Stathers," a man who was loosely associated with the church through his daughter's involvement with the youth program, but who knew Al well. On that bitterly cold Christmas Eve, we traced Al through his bread route to White River Junction, VT. We checked every possible lead, plus the Hotel Coolidge with no success. Finally we visited the Greyhound Terminal and were told that a man fitting Al's description had bought a ticket and embarked on a bus going to New York City. It was up to the Lord, now, to bring him home! Well, Al did come home and it was the turning point in his life when shortly after that he received Christ as his Savior.

Both he, Edna, and later Sandy were saved and became faithful members of Calvary Baptist. After he found the Lord, Al found just the right job for himself as the front counter man at Lavalley Building Supply. He worked there for many years until his retirement and became a valued member of the Board of Directors at Singing Hills Christian Fellowship. Sandy later became the treasurer. So the gospel message worked just the way it should—passed from person to person! A special personal friendship developed between our family and theirs and lasted to the end of Al and Edna's life. They developed a testimony for God that was a joy and encouragement through all of my ministries.

Sandy Otten Fowler served for many years as Treasurer of Singing Hills.

The way God chooses to speak to each person is no doubt unique, but in my case, as in others mentioned previously, it came as a growing feeling that I couldn't suppress. Coming toward the end of that eighth year in Claremont with the church established and growing, many new Christians and a new building almost completed, I was sensing a feeling that it was my time to move on.

Besides the miraculous way God moved within the church there were other experiences that stand out in my mind. There was the "angel" experience. One Wednesday night in the winter, I was driving the two lane country road from Claremont to Unity, NH, to pick up the Loiselle family to bring them to prayer meeting. They had come to Christ when Jack Wyrtzen spoke at the Claremont Opera House. There was a hairpin curve in the road that I knew about but was approaching at the 40 mph speed limit. My headlights were shining ahead into the woods just before the curve. I noticed what appeared to be a red light or reflector just inside the woods. My reaction to the red light was to slow down and as I rounded the corner, I came upon a disabled car having no lights and with the driver in front of it, looking under the hood. I was barely able to stop. What had happened? I went back several times trying to simulate that experience but never again saw the red light. Was this God's special way of protecting me and the man with the broken down car? I believe it was!

The apostle Paul wrote that "the people who do not know Christ do not understand spiritual things and they are foolishness to them." In my case, in regard to making life-changing decisions I would feel a kind "nudging" deep inside. In Elijah's case, perhaps that is what was meant when after spectacular displays of God's power in nature, "he heard a still, small voice from within his heart." It was then that he received his mission for the rest of his life. It is not an easy or momentous time for pastors, missionaries, or other Christian workers, or even Christian families to make life-changing decisions. My eight years at Calvary Baptist had been exciting and successful, but in the eighth year I began to feel that something was moving me on. At the time, Woodie and Trudy Style were coming to church. They had recently sold a jewelry store in Islip Long Island and purchased a beautiful building with 1,500 feet of frontage on Lake Sunapee.

Seminole Point Lodge served as a Christian vacation place for many years.

At the same time a group of three deacons from the First Baptist Church in Windsor, VT, contacted me and asked if they could come for a visit to seek advice. When we met they confided that their church was in a critical situation. Their pastor had left, taking some members with him, leaving the church divided and with few people still attending.

Now Woodie and Trudy Style had planned that their beautiful lodge on Sunapee would be just a vacation spot for Christians. I personally thought it could be much more than that for the Lord. I remember well meeting with Woodie on the boathouse roof one evening and challenging him to make the lodge a place, not just for Christians to take a vacation, but for winning souls to Christ. Our conversation ended with Woodie offering to make me "Director" of the lodge with the task of finding the groups to come and use it. They had named the property "Seminole Point Lodge."

God's Call to Begin Things

While this was happening, I had indicated to the Windsor group that I might be able to come as part-time pastor for one year to try to pull the church together and begin to build it up again. I indicated that I would be dividing my time between Windsor and Sunapee. As interim pastor in Windsor, I would have a very small salary plus use of the parsonage and when in Sunapee (weather permitting) we could spend some nights at our cottage, which was not far from there.

The year at Seminole Point was interesting but confusing to me. I was successful in finding and scheduling retreat groups, but there always seemed to be a lingering question about my future there. After I had filled the schedule, my time seemed to be taken up doing grounds work and just ministering to Woodie and Trudy and their young son, Paul.

But some humorous things happened, too. That summer, Marian and I together with Woodie and Trudy went for a ride in his newly purchased plywood outboard motor boat. He liked to think of himself as a kind of daredevil and we were doing all kinds of twists and turns in the new boat, when, "Woodie," I yelled, "watch out for that post!" The post was a marker warning for underwater rocks. Too late! "Crunch," and suddenly there was a hole in the bow, fortunately above the water line.

The other incident happened in the winter. On Lake Sunapee, three inches of clear ice was considered to be enough for ice skating or ice fishing. We were preparing for a group to come in the next day and there had been some light snow, so after Woodie and Trudy had gone to bed, I was going to shovel an area for skating. That day, Woodie had bought a brand new red Buick station wagon. What a beauty! I had borrowed the key to shine the headlights on the area I was clearing. The slight slope where I parked the car gave perfect light for my project and I put the car in "Park." Everything was going great until, "Oh, NO!" The car was beginning to roll down onto the three-inch ice and it did, right out onto the lake! I still remember going to the upstairs bedroom, knocking sheepishly on their bedroom door and sharing the news with them that their brand new Buick was out on the lake. Trudy prayed, I'm sure, while Woodie and I carefully pulled the Buick back onto solid ground.

In 1962, Marian and I were invited to attend and speak at Calvary Baptist's Tenth Anniversary. Someone had prepared a small booklet recording events of those first ten years. I was humbled and amazed at how the Lord had moved, both in the church and in our family life. The events of those eight years from 1951 to 1959 were not just great spiritual statistics. Our lives were filled with other things, too. Fred Morrison became our youth leader, and being from Pennsylvania, he was an avid hunter. So it was inevitable that he would introduce me to the sport that would entice me to the woods every fall.

Calvary Baptist Church on Maple Avenue in Claremont, NH, still has a thriving ministry.

I went hunting with Fred on the very first day of deer season, with a rifle I had never shot, one with open sights. It was bitter cold with snow on the ground. Fred and I decided to separate and while I proceeded up a logging road, he followed a small parallel stream. Our hunt had begun at the Haynes farm, just off the Charlestown Road near Claremont. I recall shivering from the cold, but all that was forgotten when I suddenly spotted a deer some distance ahead of me. As I fired, the deer jumped and ran off. However, when I reached the spot, there was blood on the snow and I knew that deer was wounded. I was determined to find it. Believe it or not, I tracked that deer for two days and late on the second day, toward dusk, I was rewarded by seeing the doe again in a clump of small fir trees and hurrying to the spot, I found her laying there where she had fallen. I got down in the snow to dress the deer and having done that I procceded to lose my hunting knife in the snow. By that time it was pitch dark. Where was I?

I suddenly realized that I was lost and it wasn't a happy thought. Thank you, Lord, that I caught a glimpse of a car's headlights through the thick young pines. That meant a road! I headed for it, pulling the deer. I was almost four miles from the Haynes farm, but I got a ride from another hunter with a pickup truck.

Ed Tierney was another member of the church who loved hunting, particularly, ruffed grouse, so I accompanied him with a shotgun again to the Haynes' farm. I was startled the first time a grouse took off. The fluttering wings and sudden take off made quite a racket. There was not a chance of my hitting it!

The reason for sharing these and other hunting stories, later, is because those diversions were truly important to me as events and responsibilities continued to multiply in my life. Marian wasn't very happy when I started bringing home the results of my hunts, especially the grouse and rabbits. I had convinced her that we should try some new, nature-provided food every week and this worked until I brought home a gray squirrel. That, together with the live lobster looking at her from the boiling water, put a screeching halt to the whole experiment. From then on it was just venison! I made a promise not to shoot any bird or animal that we would not eat or give to a needy family.

One other notable event happened when Marian was cooking a meal that consisted of tomato sauce and something else. This bright red, sticky combination was being cooked in a pressure cooker, when suddenly it exploded and sent that whole dinner onto the kitchen ceiling! Could all these things be part of a Christian life? Yes, just like sickness and health, rain and sunshine, good days and bad—all of it is called "living." And there are deeper things to deal with, too, as we will see.

Sometimes we do things that we don't think we can do! Upon remembering the years at Calvary Baptist, two special things stand out among the many other blessings, both of them were new to me and I think they launched me on a life of "starting things." My first wedding was a double one with the two grooms acting as best man for each other and the brides likewise acting as bridesmaids for each other. Betty Cummings and Irving Bruce and Elsa Bruce and Ed Tierney entrusted tying the knot to me. So with the exchanges of vows and rings, I did and they did!

The other event was my first baptism. Eighteen believers were baptized in Crescent Lake. Included among them were Mr. and Mrs. Robert Bruce who were in their 80s. Several days before the baptism, Mrs. Bruce timidly approached me to ask if it would be alright for her to take an Anacin tablet before the service. Neither she nor Mr. Bruce had been in outdoor lake water for years. I replied, "Of course it's okay." So, on it went and the only other incident occurred when Barbara Killoran tried to inhale during the "dip" and came up coughing and wheezing. So many

This house and barn was step one in developing the Maple Avenue property.

things happened in those first eight years. Much of it was recounted in a special brochure made up to celebrate the tenth year anniversary.

There were many statistics in addition, including the purchase of the property on Maple Avenue, an eight-room house with two baths and an attached garage and a barn that was renovated for use as a chapel to serve the interim period while the church building was being constructed next door.

In regard to spiritual achievements, the following are excerpts from that brochure:

"TO GOD BE THE GLORY"

1. Soon after Pastor Biebel arrived, he instituted a weekly newsletter called "Abundant Blessings."
2. In July the hour of service was changed to Sunday mornings.
3. The Pastor organized a fellowship of teenagers in the Twin State Valley that grew so that at times 175 would be present. Many were brought to Christ and some have given their lives to His service.
4. Some statistics from the first years: Sunday school, 64; Morning worship, 75; Evening worship, 90; prayer meetings, 25. There had been 98 decisions for Christ and eight of them had been baptized and joined the church.
5. At Easter time, a big rally was held at the Claremont City Hall with Jack Wyrtzen of Word of Life Fellowship. A large crowd attended and 48 more people accepted Christ. Thirteen were later baptized as a testimony to their faith.
6. In October a children's' rally was held and about 40 decisions were made, some who are now members of our church.
7. "Valley Praises" was a fifteen minute radio program originating

from WTSV in Claremont. The theme song was "I've Discovered the Way of Gladness." It was sung by a mixed quartet: Bucky Hoyt, Barbara Killoran, Ray Mark, and Betty Cummings.

8. January 4, 1956 was the day God made possible the purchase of the large house and barn adjacent to the church building lot. Within three weeks, the barn had been renovated and services held there, moving from the Odd Fellows Hall.

9. On May 7 an estimated 100 members and friends, including Claremont's Mayor, Rev. James Stuart of Concord, and Rev Nelson from Franklin, NH, arrived for the ground-breaking of the new church. That was followed on May 11 with the arrival of a bulldozer to dig the foundation area. By the middle of August the entire foundation was completed.

10. A pictorial feature story was printed in the *New York Times*, depicting the work in the woods and on the structure. A complete pictorial story about the volunteer work and building was presented in the *New Hampshire Profiles* magazine. It was done by Hanson Carroll, a professional photographer.

11. One of the outstanding events of 1958 was the laying of the church cornerstone by Dr. Myron Cederholm, President of CBA of America.

12. The fall of 1959 brought sadness to the hearts of the people when the Pastor tendered his resignation.

Our son, Paul, arrived in 1953. Right from the beginning, he's been an outdoorsman.

In addition to these facts from the brochure, I have some additional personal memories of those years. One was the arrival of the last two members of our family, Paul on Feb 16, 1953 and Judy, our only daughter on

God's Call to Begin Things

June 7, 1957. How can we ever praise the Lord enough for the gift of our wonderful family? Judy decided to come in a hurry one night. We got Marian in our car and took off for Claremont Hospital. I took the shortcut but forgot that there was a railroad crossing over the road that provided a huge bump. Fortunately, Judy waited!

Another special memory of those years was the times our family spent at our cottage on Baptist Pond. Considering the pace of events in Claremont, we badly needed that diversion.

By the spring of 1958, the church construction was well underway with our people doing much of the work. Rudy Marek, a local carpenter, was hired and served as the facilitator of the plan and to keep everything moving. I had a deep respect for Rudy, even though, as far as I know, he was not a "born again" Christian when the project started.

Rudy Marek oversaw the construction of Calvary Baptist Church, but he always had time for my sons.

While the volunteers, including the ladies, who kept the food supply coming, were important, it was Rudy and his two sons, Pete and Ted, who were the main movers to keep the work going. I was always on hand, too. Soon the foundation was laid with ten-foot cement walls. At the same time, about twelve square cement piers had been laid on the sand floor of the future basement. We were ready to start framing the superstructure and built a "walk around" made of planks so we could bring supplies and work from them on the framing.

One day, I was walking around the planks, pushing a large contractor's wheelbarrow when suddenly the plank (not being placed on the support) gave way and down I went, ten feet! I landed on my back in the sand and after catching my breath, looked up to see that I had barely missed the sharp edge of one of the cement piers. The wheelbarrow was right above me, still on the walkway but it provided an incentive to quickly move. Meanwhile, Ray Mark, who had been volunteering, ran over to the parsonage next door and said to Marian, "I think we've lost him." She remembers it well.

As for Rudy and his boys, I'm pretty sure that all three received Christ during a series of meetings we called "Echoes of Calvary." Rudy died several years later from multiple sclerosis, but I will never forget the two of us working on those forty-foot roof rafters (2 x 8s and 2 x10s) made of wet hemlock. Each connecting timber had to have a round hole drilled and a steel split ring inserted. We did all that in the dead of winter. Rudy was a master at using block and tackle to raise these very heavy roof supports into place. Finally, after the building framing was completed and windows and doors put in place, it was decided that Larry Mark would do the brick veneer. The first services were held in the basement in April 1958, with a capacity attendance.

No, that's not a cigar in my mouth! I guess I was trying to be the original nail gun.

WINDSOR

The time was coming to pack up the kids and our somewhat meager household things and move the ten miles from Maple Avenue in Claremont, NH, to the big parsonage in Windsor, VT. Little did I know it, but my commitment of one year would turn into thirteen!

As I became the pastor of the First Baptist Church, my first challenge was to appraise the situation. It was pretty bleak! The former pastor had split the church, left, and taken members with him. The remaining ones were left with feelings of insecurity and some ill will. The attendance had dropped to just a few families and individuals. But I found the remaining ones to be solid Christians and good individuals. What to do?

The First Baptist Church in Windsor

One of my first messages was taken from Philippians 3:13, "Forgetting those things which are behind, and reaching forth unto the things that are ahead, I press toward the mark, for the prize of the high calling of God in Christ Jesus." I stated that, as pastor, I did not want to become involved at all in any of the past controversies and I asked the remaining people to follow my lead.

To me, personal communication has always been the answer and while there were no cell phones or Internet in those days, we did have telephones and mimeographs. James says, in Scripture, that sometimes the Lord sends testing to build our faith. The liquid-operated mimeograph provided me with many a test, but we did use it to get the word out about our programs and to publish some sermons. We had an ever-expanding mailing list. We decided, too, as in Claremont that ten percent of the church's income would go to missions. I initiated a pre-service prayer meeting, asking the deacons and deaconesses to attend. It was held in the small room adjacent to the pulpit area. I also visited as many families as possible. Things began to happen!

It didn't take me long to become aware that, once again, the Holy Spirit was nudging me, and a short time later, I resigned my job at Seminole

Point Lodge to become totally involved with the Windsor church, and as it turned out, also with the community. So, for me, it was time out to seek the Lord's guidance for the future in Windsor. My desire to do His will was uppermost, so where would I start? I never put values on what should come first, believing that all the phases of my life were part of one plan, God's! My family was part of his plan and I needed to take care of them. Fortunately we had a large parsonage on Route 5 (Main Street) across from the church. It was a very big old house with stairs everywhere and rooms for everyone. My starting salary with the church was small, out of necessity, but thanks to Marian's working, we were able to have a good lifestyle with enough of everything. She was Medical Assistant to Dr. Michael Daly for several years and then when he had to retire because of ill health, she worked as a secretary at Cone Automatic Machine Company, which was within walking distance of our home.

As for the church itself, it needed help both spiritually and materially. The sanctuary needed painting as did the rest of the building. That posed a big problem because of the diminished attendance. It was obvious that I, together with those who believed in the future, needed to get to work. I had a lot to learn, too, about Windsor. It was an old town with stores lining the main street but also had interesting other areas. Goodyear Company had a factory in town as did the Cone Automatic Machine Company. In the aftermath of World War II, these two plants provided employment for many of the residents, including some of our church members.

The State Street School housed the elementary grades and there was also the "Humpty Dumpty Kollege," a privately owned and operated preschool where we enrolled Judy. We went to her graduation and didn't know it at the time but our future daughter-in-law, Kathie Bartlett, also graduated that day. Other features of Windsor included Paradise Park, the Vermont State Prison, the Fairgrounds, and Kennedy's Pond. These would all have a part in my life in the next thirteen years.

Mary and Emma Sanderson were sisters who had never married. Their family had a long history in the church and two of the stained glass windows were dedicated to past family members. These two sisters were special in a number of ways, faithfulness being the most important. They always sat together and sometimes chatted quietly during my messages, shaking their heads yes or no, always in unison, indicating agreement or disagreement with what I was saying.

One of the first physical challenges was our project to paint the inside of the church. Leading the way as a pastor should, I began on the back wall. I placed a ladder against the wall, forgetting that the floor underneath was hardwood with varnish. Taking the full pail of paint up with me, I was almost to the top when, "OH NO!" The bottom was slipping. Down went the ladder, me, and the full gallon of paint. The can landed upright but the beige-colored paint went shooting up into the air like a geyser, and where did it go? Well, you guessed it, right on the Sanderson's stained glass window and over the last two rows of pews. So, our project became one of cleaning up but we did finish the painting after the pause.

Now that we were in Windsor, I still had memories of Claremont. One was of a little girl, Linda Staff, who had attended Daily Vacation Bible School and received the Lord as Savior there. Her mother, Joan had given us our first dog, Andy, who was a full-blooded black Labrador Retriever. What a dog he was! Being a born retriever, he had gone around the neighborhood in Claremont and returned home bringing items he had collected from neighbors. Now in Windsor, we had to curtail those expeditions and it was a sad day when Andy, dying of cancer, had to go for a last visit to the vet. But that in turn introduced a whole series of dogs into our family. Sandy was a Border Collie mix that turned out to be one of our best and smartest. There was another, Mandy, who had a very short stay. Mandy was not very smart and had a habit of getting right up on the kitchen table and eating out of the sugar bowl. One day he went running out the front door and into the traffic and was hit by a pickup. That was it!

For Sandy, her adventure had almost the same ending. Our son, Paul, had made a room for himself way up in the attic and had fixed it up with an old easy chair, right by an open window—great for ventilation on hot nights. Sandy liked Paul and also liked that chair and often slept in it. One night, I came home from a meeting and was heading up the stairs to our bedroom. Out of the corner of my eye, I saw something furry plummet past the living room window. *Oh, no, could that be Sandy? She'll be dead for sure!* I thought, hastening outside and around the corner of the house to see Sandy standing there with a very dazed look on her face. She had fallen about twenty feet from that attic window and bounced off the rounded cover of the bottled propane gas container. A quick trip to the vet showed that her only wound was some scraped off hair on her rump. But she did get some notoriety. In those days one of TV's popular series was "The Flying Nun." The next day the local paper carried a story entitled, "Sandy the Flying Dog."

I think Paul was born with a train in his cradle, so it was fitting that we would have railroad tracks just over the bank in our backyard. Trains always blew their whistle as they approached the crossing nearby and the freight trains were long and pretty slow. We wouldn't know it for many years but Paul almost hitched a ride on one of those going north to White River Jct., VT. The ultimate destination was Montreal. His love of trains, particularly Lionel, stuck with him always. He's even found ways to integrate this avocation into his vocation as a General Contractor.

Paul's company uses a fabulous train display to educate kids and adults about energy sources and uses.

Right next to our house was Bud Richards' gas station, where sometimes he had used cars for sale. Bud was a good guy and on many occasions allowed folks attending our church to park in his station, which was closed on Sundays. Once he had two "Simcas" for sale. The deal was quite persuasive. These were cars made in France and were supposed to get fifty miles per gallon. There were two big problems that led to much frustration on our part. First, they were allergic to temperatures under 40 degrees and would not start when it was cold, which it is a good part of the year in Vermont, of course. Secondly, the stick shifts made a crunching sound every time you tried to shift and if you rested your hand on the stick it would slip right into neutral. Oh, well, we gave them a try but they just had to "go" after a short stay.

As mentioned before, the parsonage was a huge house; it actually had four levels. The basement was unfinished and mostly unused. As in all of my ministries, I had a special concern for the youth. We already had a pretty good start with a youth group with our own four children, but almost as soon as we came to Windsor, our youth program began to grow. What then could we do to replace "Teen Time Ranch," the youth center we had established during our ministry in Claremont? We decided to give up the sanctity of our home and make that huge downstairs into a youth center. With the help of some of the older men, together with the older boys, twenty-two and a half tons of cement was poured, which Stuart Shepard turned into a smooth surface floor using a power trowel. It wasn't until much later that Stuart made it known that whenever he used that machine indoors, he ended up with a migraine headache. But that is the kind of commitment that our people had to reaching the youth of our town.

Quoting from a church newsletter of that year: "Since then, a ceiling has been added, rest rooms have been completed, a heating system has been installed, walls have been painted or covered with beautiful wallboard, and many other things accomplished, all on a pay-as-we-go basis. For several weeks, the Center has been open each afternoon to the younger teens and on weeknights to the older teens."

Those who thought they were still teenagers like the older men Charlie Byron, John Knisley, and Perley Bowen came to try their skills at pool. The schedule was: Friday night—BYF, or Young Life as it was called; Saturday evening—"Teenagers;" Monday night—the Christian Fish and Game Club. Thus the basement of our home become a beehive of activity and many found Christ in the meetings, which always had a spiritual message.

Mike and Alice Hamblen had originally come to our area under the auspices of Word of Life to try to establish "Word of Life" Bible clubs in our area. We were impressed with their commitment, but they left and returned to Tennessee Temple University to complete their college studies. We asked them to come back after graduation to be our church youth leaders.

God's Call to Begin Things

One of my favorite ladies of all time, excluding Marian and daughter, Judy, was Mrs. Mabel Hurd. She was a very faithful deaconess, and always present at the pre-service prayer meetings, sometimes being the only one with me. She had special qualities that affected me personally. She showed love and concern for everyone in spite of the fact that her personal family life had many problems. I was impressed with the way she dealt with her adult son's uncontrolled bouts with epilepsy, which frequently occurred during church services, but rarely caused a disruption. She was a Registered Nurse and served as the First Aid person for the employees at the Cone Automatic Machine Co. She instituted a prayer meeting with the employees once a week during the noontime break. She was greatly respected by the company and its employees. When she retired, one of the employees wrote the following poem in her honor:

Mabel Hurd was a rare example of what Christian love can accomplish at home and work.

OUR THOUGHTS

We think of one who was faithful in placing the chairs.
We think of the fellowship we had in many prayers.
We remember the times we looked into His Word,
And the friendly greeting from you, Mrs. Hurd.
We remember a good nurse who cares.

You're concern for sick friends and events now and then,
But most of us notice your dedication when:

It comes time to mention the prayer request,
The one we all remember best
Was your "Don't forget to pray for the Safety of the Men."

The Lord only knows how much your labor brings to fruition,
What blessings may have come from the clippings for admonition
How many have read receiving the witness,
That along with your concern for our physical fitness,
You also had thoughts about the soul's condition.

Now in your retirement, we can see you won't be bored,
As you avail your life to all God can afford.
We anticipate the next chapter of the story,
God supplying all your need according to His riches in glory.
We of the Prayer Group covet for you happiness in the Lord.

Author Anon

It was Mrs. Hurd who came speeding onto the fairgrounds while I was playing softball, to tell me that our church was on fire. All of us who were playing that day clearly had heard the town's fire whistle. The number of times the whistle blew indicated approximately where the fire was located. Our parsonage was right next to a gas station and next to that was the Unitarian church. In the front stairway of that church there had been a plaque reading "The Fatherhood of God and the Brotherhood of Man." At some point, this sign got the goat of some of the atheist members and it was removed. I thought that the Lord must be angry about this. So, when the fire whistle blew, I was pretty sure that it had to be that Unitarian church. Instead, it was ours!

The fire in the church turned out to be from an electrical panel room in the rear of the church and fortunately the flames went directly up and through the roof. Although limited in damage to the structure, thick, dark smoke permeated the entire building. When flowing out through the baptistry at the front of the sanctuary, the smoke formed what looked like an angel.

As for me, when I got to the church, Bill Buchanan, the fire chief, said I could go in to rescue the big Bible and other items from the pulpit area. At the time, I was dressed in a bright green softball uniform with the sponsor's name on the back. As I exited the church, my eyes were watering from the acidic fumes and I was covered in black soot. The next day the local paper carried a front page picture of me carrying the Bible and communion plates out of the building, and my image was not edited. But the fire turned out to be a blessing in disguise! With some insurance coverage and help from other churches, we were able to completely renovate the upstairs sanctuary and balcony. In the meantime, we met in the downstairs auditorium.

Speaking of the baptistry, one other relatively hilarious event occurred when I attempted to baptize a fellow who was maybe six foot eight, who kept his legs straight the first time I tried to get him underwater. "Bill," I whispered, "bend your knees!" And when he did, it all worked out.

Mrs. Edna Beaulmont was another of the godly women of our church and her daughter and son-in-law were Evelyn and Scotty Olechnowicz. Their son, Scot, had enlisted in the Navy and served on one of the earlier nuclear submarines. Scot came home after discharge from the Navy, and shortly after, was attending a bachelor party for a friend who was getting married. After the party, a friend was driving an open jeep with Scot as passenger. As they were coming down a steep hill, the driver lost control, went down an embankment and slammed into a white birch tree. Scot was launched from his seat and thrown against the tree with his whole body. Almost every bone was broken and he was rushed by ambulance to Mary Hitchcock Hospital in Hanover, NH, where he underwent eight hours of surgery with his life hanging by a thread. To make things worse, he received an emergency blood transfusion that did not match his blood type. He was going to die, or so they thought!

Evelyn and Scotty were urged to come to the hospital immediately but in the meantime, Mrs. Beaulmont called me and said, "Pastor, please go and pray for Scot and anoint him with oil as it says in Scripture, in the book of James, "... and the prayer of faith will heal the sick and if he has committed sins, they will be forgiven." I was the first to arrive at Scot's bedside. He was unconscious. I leaned over, praying that if it was God's will, he would spare Scot. I anointed him with some cooking oil that I had hastily taken from our kitchen.

On the way to the hospital, I had paused, pulling over beside the road to settle an issue in my own life: Did I really believe the promise? When I arrived, all Scot's signs were in negative territory. His parents had not yet arrived, but by the time they did, all his vital signs had changed to positive—blood pressure, respiration, and the rest. The rest of the story is that Scot fully recovered, went to college and married. I lost track of him, but then one Christmas he sent me a card signed, "Thanks, Scot."

Early in my ministry in Windsor, another door opened to me unexpectedly! The Congregational Pastor in Windsor had been the part-time Chaplain at the Vermont State Prison, but he was leaving Windsor. For some unexplained reason he recommended me for the sixteen-hour-a week job. In addition to the opportunity to reach the inmates and security staff with the gospel, the added income was a welcome boon to our family. During the next six years I discovered just how evil human beings can be, but at the same time, I saw how Jesus can work even in the darkest life. I had an office adjacent to the visiting room where "trustees" could visit. Next to my office on one side was the Catholic Chaplain's office and on the other side was a dentist's room. All these were glassed. Across the large visiting area was another small

God's Call to Begin Things

I served for six years as Protestant Chaplain of the Vermont State Prison, built in 1847. It's now the "Olde Windsor Village Apartments."

room where a state-employed psychiatrist occasionally visited. Also, in that area were several inmates, including one named Fred, who produced a prison monthly newsletter named "The Green Mountain Graphic." One part of my job was to interview all the Protestant inmates and prior to the visit, I was to read their presentencing and trial results, a very unpleasant but necessary task. Since this was a maximum security prison, there were murderers, sex offenders, robbers, and perpetrators of every bad thing you could think of!

The warden, Bob Smith, had warned me to be careful and always alert to someone wanting to get me. He was a good man, but especially nervous at times. But in my six years of service, I was never menaced in any way. I had two policies with the inmates coming through my office. One, I was there to minister to them spiritually and two, unless they told me the truth from the beginning, coming to see me would be a waste of time. In spite of Warden Smith's warning, I tried to gain their respect. During "Yard Time" I would go out and shoot baskets and when possible would play softball at probably the most unique field ever. The makeshift rules included doubles and home runs based on which building or wall you hit. Later, I was able to get the warden to permit carefully screened inmates to enter a team in the town softball league and that proved to be successful—no problems!

The warden approached the Catholic chaplain and me about arranging a Christmas party for the inmates. We were to get together with a small committee of "trustee" inmates to plan the program, which would be held in the chapel. The prison itself had been built in 1847, the oldest in the USA, and was surrounded by thirty foot walls with guard houses on each corner, overlooking the "yard." The chapel was in the same building as the dining area and was directly above the kitchen, a real fire hazard (a hundred years of kitchen grease). At any rate, we proceeded with plans and the committee decided that for music they wanted "Woodie and the Ramblers," a country type band, consisting of about four people. Woodie himself was a huge man.

Before the event took place, the other chaplain excused himself and I was left to be the Master of Ceremonies. When the day arrived and I was in the chapel with Woodie's band, there was a "rumble" in the cell blocks. The inmates were yelling and banging whatever they could on the cell bars. Should the party go ahead? The decision made by the Associate Warden was, yes! As Woodie and his group and I were on the platform, over two hundred disgruntled inmates were ushered in, accompanied by eight guards armed only with wooden clubs. This was definitely a situation for me to ask for God's help, which I did.

When the men were seated, I took the microphone and said something like, "Men, this is a special time when we celebrate Jesus' birth and we need to have a good spirit." Then, I turned to Woodie and said, "Start playing." And when they did, the inmates settled down and the rest of the party went well. There was cake and ice cream and the whole situation had changed for the better.

As I was preparing to leave, I noticed a young man, Paul, who was standing by a window. I had met with him a number of times. He was good looking and intelligent—a cut above some of the others. I noticed that there were tears in his eyes as he said to me, "I made a big mistake and I am going to do better." After his release he went to Rhode Island and worked in the school system. Some time later, I received a note from the school superintendent, complimenting Paul for his work and thanking me.

During my six years as prison chaplain, there were many incidents, but two or three stand out in my memory. Although the job was part-time, I was on call 24/7, and when there was a crisis, the warden didn't hesitate to have the chaplains called. One frigid winter night I was called and told that I was needed ASAP! Two of the younger inmates had somehow gotten to the roof of the building used for reconditioning furniture, a job that certain inmates could do to earn a small hourly wage (ten cents). When I arrived at the prison the warden was in the entry room, anxiously pacing back and forth and watching events unfold out of the window. The fire chief and his men had come through the huge prison gate and had set up their engine in the yard. Using a loud speaker, the men were warned to come down and instructed to strip. They refused at first, but when the firemen turned the hose on them in the sub-zero weather, they came down in a big hurry with icicles hanging from their bodies.

On another occasion, I was called at night to come—there was an urgent situation! "John," an eighteen-year-old inmate was in his cell threatening to set himself on fire. He had somehow obtained a flammable liquid. I had met with John, which we all knew was not his real name. Several times he claimed to have worked at Word of Life Ranch, taking care of the horses. When I arrived at the cell block, I approached his cell and saw that he was highly agitated emotionally and his hair and clothes were in disarray. I had a policy throughout my chaplaincies of "calmness" no matter the circumstances and I said something like, "C'mon John, let's talk about it and find out what's the matter." He responded to my approach and told me that the guards in his cell block had been harassing him and they had taken away his TV. He calmed down when I said I would help if I could. Looking into the matter, I found that there was some truth to his story and reported it to the warden, who corrected the situation.

Another time, the warden and I were on our way to Burlington, VT, for a conference and I discussed with him that some of the guards were deliberately inciting the inmates. They would notice that an inmate had a pretty woman visiting and then would incite him by saying, "It's going to be great visiting with your wife tomorrow night." That practice stopped but the interaction between guards and inmates, except for a few of the guards, was risky, if not hostile.

My chaplaincy at the prison lasted for six years and several things stick in my memory. Walt R was a most unusual inmate in that he was the only one to ever make it over the wall in an attempted escape. The only thing was, in jumping down the other side, which was thirty feet high, he broke his leg. After that healed and he established his reliability, he was allowed to go with the delivery truck that returned completed reupholstered furniture to various locations. On one such trip, Walt walked away and stole some wire that had been left at an electric company site. He was quickly returned to prison but confided to me that he deliberately did it so he could be rearrested and returned to prison. He said, "I can't make it on the outside!"

In a somewhat similar circumstance, a little man in his late middle age was released after a number of years being incarcerated. He was given clothes, a stipend, and good wishes from the warden. He had served his time. Two days later, he was found sitting on the stairs of the administration building with tears in his eyes and begging to get back in. The world outside was too much for him.

There was a young man, Norm, who was doing time for stealing a car. He was good looking and very smart. I spent time sharing the gospel with him and although he was Catholic, he came to my office. Norm had a positive future. Sometime after his release he met a very attractive and somewhat wealthy woman and together, after marrying, they purchased and operated several ski and clothing stores in Boston and Vermont. Before that, however, Norm had appeared at my door at the parsonage one night and asked to see me. As we talked, he said, "There's an All-Points Bulletin out for me. They're claiming I stole another car and I didn't do it. What shall I do?" My advice was to go down, on his own, to see the warden, and that is what he did.

God's Call to Begin Things

I need to say at least something positive about the inmates and guards. There were some inmates who genuinely wanted to change their lives and there were some who were writing regularly to a Korean orphan named Vu Su. As for the prison staff, they had a project to furnish Christmas gifts for the inmates' children.

The prison newsletter, "Green Mountain Graphic," included some inspirational thoughts by certain men. The warden and associate warden, Mike O'Hara, did their best to keep at least an even atmosphere in a very tough environment.

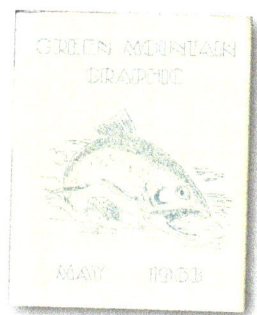

I often wrote outdoor stories for the Prison newsletter, each with a devotional thought.

Those first years at First Baptist in Windsor from 1960-1965 passed so quickly. I was becoming more involved in community affairs, especially with the youth. I organized a hockey program in the winters and coached Little League—the Red Sox team of course—in the summer. When the time came to pick from the potential players, of course I picked my own sons. On one occasion, Bob Smith, the prison warden was the umpire and when he called a pitch that went over the boy's head a strike, I ran out to question the call. He told me to get back to the bench or he would toss me. What a dilemma it would be for the warden to throw out the chaplain. In spite of it all,

I worked hard to keep the hockey rink ice in shape. And sometimes we got to play. Dave (left), me (center), and Dan in goal.

we (the Red Sox) had a really good team and won a lot of games. Sons Dave and Dan were standouts with Dan catching, against his will, and Dave hitting home runs. He held the all-time record of twenty homers in that year. The windows of several parked cars parked behind the fence had been broken.

As for the hockey team, we established a rink at the Fairgrounds where most outdoor sports were held. I scoured the businesses in town and raised the money needed to put fences around the rink and purchased some uniforms along with sticks and pucks.

At about that time, the town manager and the town council appointed me the "volunteer town recreation chairman." A piece written in a local newspaper *The Valley News* described my job, dated October 16, 1963. "Rev. Biebel came to Windsor in 1959 as minister of the First Baptist Church and he is also serving as Protestant chaplain at the Vermont State Prison. In addition to his outstanding work for his church, Rev. Biebel has been very active in the organization of the Windsor Recreation Committee, a group of which he is chairman and under whose guidance several sports programs have been initiated and carried out. Rev. Biebel is also active in the Calvin Coolidge Council of Boy Scouts and a member of the executive council."

This treasured award from the Jaycees recognized my work as Chair of the Windsor Recreation Committee.

The occasion for this article was an award I treasure greatly. It was, "The award for special service to the community by a junior citizen." It was nice to receive the award but being chairman of the committee included doing most of the work. The hockey rink at the Fairgrounds was on a level patch of ground, but it wasn't long before I found out that the earth underneath the surface was mostly gravel, not the best for holding water. We (the youth team) were playing scheduled games with Claremont and others who had teams, as well as adult men's teams from the area. So, getting a decent ice surface required my being out at the rink, sometimes late in the evening trying to fill and freeze the pockets where the water underneath had seeped away before freezing. Fortunately, I had the help of our fire chief, who provided fire hose and opened a hydrant for water. After finishing in below zero temperatures, a warm house and a cup of hot chocolate never felt so good.

But, there would be much more community work to come! It is not easy for a pastor, passionate to win people to Christ, to also become involved in community affairs. My prayer and objective in doing so always kept my priority in living for and serving Christ, and that my time in Windsor would open many doors to minister to people, and it did.

As both the church and the youth groups began to grow, transportation became a problem and we were able to buy a secondhand school bus. Bud, our next door gas station owner, allowed us to park the bus in an area behind the station. That bus would put on lots of miles to many activities and was always accompanied by plenty of happy noise and singing!

As pastor, I was kept busy visiting parishioners and prospective members, as well as preparing for the services. The youth program was growing by leaps and bounds and many decisions were made for Christ. Mike and Alice Hamblen had returned and were doing a great job as our youth leaders and their home provided a welcome place for the teens in addition to the youth center in our house. Initial plans were made for special trips and other programs.

One big project was to prepare for a trip to Montreal and the World's Fair called "Expo 67." Starting with the planning, until the day we left for the trip in the yellow bus, everything had to be considered. Tents for sleeping, rain gear (glad we had that), food, parents' permissions, and so much more. Looking back, I am amazed at the logistics involved in these trips but I am surer than ever that those events were an important part of our youth ministry. By the way, it rained almost all of the four days we were there but it didn't dampen our spirits. It was a challenge for the outdoor cook, though.

Another of the trips took extensive planning and preparation. It involved five cars and thirty people with clothes and supplies for five days. It was called "The Washington, New York Trip" and occurred June 16 through June 20, 1969. What a trip that was! The first night took us to Coatsville, PA, where we stayed at the "Old Mill Bible Conference." Besides having everything we needed, we had a retired missionary, Archie McKinley speak to us. He challenged all of us to dedicate our talents to the Lord for service. We were off to a great start! Tuesday morning, June 17, after a great breakfast and a slight delay for repairs on one of the cars, we were off for our destination, Washington, DC.

Once in Washington, our plan was to disperse into smaller groups and meet back at the Smithsonian Institute at 3:00 p.m. It's hard to envision now, but we covered a whole lot of destinations in one day: the Museum of Natural History, the Museum of History and Technology, the Aero Space Museum, the Dept. of Printing and Engraving, and the White House grounds. Some took a bus tour that included the Lincoln Memorial, Jefferson Memorial, U.S. Capitol, Dept. of Justice, the Federal Building, and the Aquarium. We had an enjoyable evening meal in the cafeteria of the Museum of History and Technology. Then it was on by foot to the Washington Monument. I was one of the few who decided to climb the 897 stairs while most chose the elevator. What a sight it was to see our nation's capital at night from the top of the monument!

On Wednesday morning, June 18, we all needed a little extra sleep and it was close to noon when we were "ship shape" and ready to leave for our next destination which was Northport, Long Island, and the home of Mr. and Mrs. Andrew Carlson, Alice Hamblen's brother and sister-in-law. There we camped out in their back yard and with the help of Hank Carlson, Alice's brother, we found our way to Kentucky Fried Chicken and purchased five barrels of chicken and French fries. Then, it was back to the beach, where we had a campfire, gave testimonies, sang, and finally turned in for the night, tired but happy!

Thursday, June 19, was a great day for all of us. We took the Long Island Railroad to New York City where we took the Circle Line boat trip around Manhattan Island, which included a full narration describing the various sights, a tour that took two hours and forty minutes. Then it was by bus to Madison Square Garden where we picked up our reserved tickets to the "Billy Graham Crusade." We were advised to go right in and find our seats, even though it was almost two hours early. The crowds were unbelievable and it was exciting to see thousands of people pushing to get in to hear the gospel. The service included a 2,500 voice choir and the singing was led by Cliff Barrows. Ethel Waters sang, as did a folk group, and several well-known people shared testimonies. The response to Billy's message was awe-inspiring. From our location in the upper balcony, so many people moving forward at the invitation made it seem like the whole building was moving. The experience was one that we'll never forget.

After supper at the Horn & Hardart Automat cafeteria, it was back on the 11:09 p.m. train to Long Island, arriving at 12:30 a.m., tired and happy!

Friday, June 20 was a beautiful morning for our trip back home to Windsor, VT. After a cookout on the beach and stuffing ourselves with barbecued hamburgers, we were ready to leave. Some of the boys fortunately discovered a bad tire on our equipment trailer and after that was changed, we all left. We had traveled 1,200 miles and through seven states and the District of Columbia. The last car arrived back home in Windsor about 10:00 p.m.

The reason I have detailed this trip in my book is that it shows the effort that we put into our youth program and why it resulted in so many teenagers coming to Christ. Twenty-four teenagers and six adults made the trip and I am quite sure that all of them know the Lord as Savior. This kind of special activity became a regular part of the church in Windsor, although not all of them were quite as large as this undertaking.

In addition to our major adventures, there were many day trips like the one we made with a bus full of teens to Rumney Bible Conference, in Rumney, NH. On the trip home, on a steep hill in Warren, NH, our school bus "Old Yellow" decided it was tired and gave up. I was a good driver but knew next to nothing about mechanical problems. Fortunately Bill Porter, one of the older teenagers, had the knowledge and magic touch to fix whatever was wrong and we were back on our way.

At the church, besides the regular services, we often had guest speakers, and among them was Pastor Stanley Allaby, pastor of Black Rock Congregational Church, my home church, in Fairfield, CT, and also Norman Clayton, the great Christian song writer and pianist. Norm wrote the beautiful hymn, "Now I Belong to Jesus." Stan's ministry was one of evangelism and was very successful, as was Norman Clayton's.

One afternoon I had asked Stan if he would like to go bow hunting with me, to watch as an observer. I had told him about a camouflaged stand I had made in the woods. There was a special place in Hartland, VT, which I had scouted and found plentiful evidence of deer. We hiked into the woods for some time trying to find my camouflaged stand, but it was so well camouflaged that I couldn't find it! So we kept hunting until we came to what looked like an ideal spot where Stan could stand on a small hill behind a tree while I was stationed along the logging road below. I was equipped with a forty-pound "Bear" long bow and six razor-tipped arrows. I carefully removed some dried leaves for a place to stand quietly, and where I could move my feet if necessary for a better angle at game that might come by.

Almost immediately I spotted some movement on the logging road directly in front of me. I signaled to Stan to be extra quiet, and waited. The medium-sized doe kept coming until she was only about twenty feet from me. My bow was ready! The problem was that she was facing me, and had stopped dead in her tracks, just standing there. Twang! I let the first arrow fly and "thud" it lodged in a small sapling that I hadn't even noticed. The doe just stood there. *How can she be so dumb?* I wondered. By the time I had emptied my quiver, and she was still there; I was the dumb one, and Stan had a great laugh.

That evening, a cartoon depicting the event mysteriously appeared in the entry way of the church, so all the incoming folks could share in the hilarity. The future though, would allow me two deer with that old fashioned bow. The services with Stan Allaby once again proved to be very successful. The church was growing spiritually and numerically.

The Adrian Devost family had a small farm in Hartland, VT, and although they had a French Catholic background, they did everything they could to help with our youth program. One Halloween, we had a funny spook walk around their barn and then had refreshments and I shared the gospel with the large group of teenagers. Years later, we received a surprise telephone call from one of their daughters who had married and was living in Concord, NH. She called to tell us that she had accepted Christ through our teenage program and was active and serving in the First Baptist Church in Concord.

As for Adrian, he was one of our key adult hockey players and we had a pretty good men's team. We were invited to play a team at Kimball Union Academy which had a covered rink and all the equipment necessary to keep the ice in good skating condition. Dr. Carver was the headmaster of KUA and his two adult sons were on the team. We played on two Saturday nights in a row. We had a great time but in the course of each evening, I received a black eye, once from an inadvertent stick and another from a puck. You can imagine the good natured remarks made by my congregation on the two following Sundays.

Proverbs 17:22 says, "A merry heart does good like a medicine." I have always believed that part of our task to be "lights in the world" includes a good sense of humor used rightly. On Sundays, I had several habits incorporated in my preaching. One was to take the opportunity while the ushers were receiving the offering, to clear my throat and blow my nose when necessary. On one particular Sunday, I stood up as the ushers were completing the offering, reached into my back pocket and pulled out—not the handkerchief, but one of Marian's long white nurse's stockings. So there I was with the choir behind me and the congregation before me with the long white stocking dangling down. Oh, well, it provided all of them with "a cheerful heart," a laugh, and gave me a story to share with you.

While I was busy 24/7, Mike and Alice Hamblen were busy, too, hosting the teenagers, having Bible studies, and other activities. But Mike did have some spare time for his favorite activity, which was flying. He became a member of the Claremont Flying Club and was eligible to rent a plane when it was available. Another person from our congregation, who also had a pilot license, was Al Catozzi. My first invitation for a flight was from Al. We would be renting the club plane and going for a spin around the Twin State Valley. So, we embarked in the two-seater plane and proceeded to the far end of the paved runway. At that point we needed to turn into the wind and to do so would mean leaving the pavement and maneuvering on the grassy strip. As we made the turn and the left wheel dropped off of the pavement, several inches, the wheel strut collapsed and thus ended our flight, but not without a few thoughts about the overall safety of the entire idea!

On another occasion, Mike invited me to fly to Boston to a baseball game. We would take off from Claremont and land at the private side of Logan airport. The flight was relatively smooth, but I kept asking Mike how we were doing. I was amazed, looking down at New Hampshire, to see how forested it is, nothing but woods and an occasional town until we were nearing Concord, Manchester, and points south toward Boston. Mike was on the radio for landing instructions and I knew he was fed up with my "anxiety" questions so I decided to keep my mouth shut. Our plan was to land, find ground transportation to Fenway Park, see the Red Sox game, and then fly home. The approach and landing were perfect but as we were turning to park the plane, I looked out and imagined that we were too close to the fence. Oops! It was too late. Crunch! The wing tip grazed the heavy wire fence and collapsed the tip. It was not a good ending to our flight. I felt bad for Mike as we took the bus ride home, but it would not be my last flight with him. My next one would be just a few years later in Florida.

There are times in life when an event suddenly happens that profoundly affects you. One such event happened on a summer's afternoon when a group of teenagers were swimming in a well-known pool, part of the Brownsville Brook. One of them was Jeff Waters, a handsome, athletic young man. But on this day Jeff made the grave mistake of diving into water that was not deep enough, breaking his neck on the rocky bottom. He was rushed to Mary Hitchcock Hospital, where it was determined that he was losing spinal fluid. When I heard about the accident, I immediately decided to visit the Waters family, who lived just off the Brownsville Road. As I drove to their home and parked in front, I wondered what I could say to help them. "Help me Lord!" I prayed. The family, whom I had known only through Little League, had received the tragic prognosis and were in a state of shock. I decided not to say much, except to put my arm around the mother and dad and say that they were loved and that all their friends would be praying for Jeff and also for them. It turned out to be the right thing to do! In the following days, I visited Jeff, who was fully conscious although his life was slowly slipping away. During one of those visits I asked Jeff if he would take Jesus into his heart and his response was, yes!

It was summer and our family was scheduled to go on vacation to Marian's parents' home in Milford, CT. Our youth leader, Mike, was a capable counselor and after a week had passed of Jeff's hospitalization, it was decided that we should proceed with our plan and leave the situation regarding Jeff with Mike. This was a time in my ministry when the Lord was teaching me that there are situations in life that we couldn't plan and this was one of them. Marian and I were enjoying our vacation but always with the situation back in Windsor on our minds. I felt sure that God could do a miracle and spare Jeff's life. What a testimony it would be to his family and to all of Windsor. I kept in touch with Mike, but had a growing restlessness about this situation, particularly with the still fresh thoughts of Scot's miraculous recovery on my mind.

> Jesus said to her, "I am the resurrection and the life; he that believeth in me, though he were dead, yet shall he live and whosoever lives and believes in me shall never die."

One evening, I decided it was time to go right to the Lord about it so I went into mom and dad's bedroom, got down on my knees and asked God for an answer. I had the Bible open and my eyes fell on John 11:14, Jesus said to her, "I am the resurrection and the life; he that believeth in me, though he were dead, yet shall he live and whosoever lives and believes in me shall never die." At that moment, I knew that Jeff had died, and was with the Lord now.

Within ten minutes the phone rang. It was Mike calling to give me the news, but I told him I already knew. Special thoughts came into my mind and I remembered the other occasions when God had answered me so directly!

God's Call to Begin Things

During the thirteen years that we ministered in Windsor, Marian and I had several special opportunities to vacation in Florida. One was an invitation from Harry and Cora Cox, who lived in Miami in a two bedroom condominium. Harry was assistant Pastor in the huge Presbyterian Church in downtown Miami across the street from Miami University. Paul McViddy, the bully who had targeted me in our junior high school days, was the pastor. How we were looking forward to that vacation break. We had boarded our Southwest flight and were flying at about thirty thousand feet when I suddenly got a hard pain in my jaws and my mouth locked shut! I had lockjaw! So, for the rest of our week, I had to drink through a straw while the others had tempting meals. We were invited to prayer meeting at the McViddy home and found a good crowd there. After the meeting, Paul asked me if I would like to play a round of golf and even with my jaw problem, my answer was yes! So we played at one of the prestigious courses located along the causeway between mainland Miami and Biscayne Island.

During the round I discovered that McViddy had remarried a beautiful girl who was one of the heirs to the McDonald Douglas Co. It wasn't until sometime after we returned to Windsor that we picked up the Boston paper to find that Paul's wife had been shot in the heart during a robbery in a supermarket in Miami. Although she survived the attack, Paul had gone on a public tirade which made the main headline in the Miami Herald stating that he would get the "Blankety-blank" guy. After that we lost touch with them but I believe that they moved to Maine. Meanwhile we returned to Windsor and I went to a dentist who put me under sedation and slowly "pried" my jaw open. So, once again I could talk and eat. Thank you, Lord!

Mike Hamblen's parents, Alta and "Captain" Hamblen, were employed by the Miami Boatyard. Captain Hamblen was the best "skipper" in Miami, even though he was hindered somewhat by lameness as the result of childhood polio. We were invited to visit them and as part of our stay we would have a sail on the boat that Captain Hamblen was operating. The "Cosa Grande" was a 115-foot-long converted Canadian Corvette, used during the war for hunting submarines. It was narrow and sleek. Many dignitaries had leased the boat for special occasions, including the making of a Hollywood movie that featured Sidney Poitier in which he was to slice a small boat in half, trying to kill the two occupants. He had to steer the boat until the very last minute and Captain Hamblen would finish the dramatic collision. The two stunt men would jump out just in time.

Our cruise out into the ocean was uneventful, except that I saw a huge fish leap out of the water, some distance away. What a splash he made! We sailed around Biscayne Island and moored for the night in Biscayne Bay, not far from President Nixon's summer home. Mike decided to pursue that fish in a small skiff so one of the crew members and I accompanied him. I had visions of what would happen if that fish I had seen took the huge bait we trolled. I was sure our skiff would be towed a long way. One of the other exciting events on that trip was when Mike rented a plane at the Miami Airport and we flew up the coast just off the beaches and Mike let me fly the plane. We flew north to Bible Town where Alice's parents, the Carlson's, owned a condominium. It was a wonderful and necessary vacation for us.

Returning to Windsor, I became involved more than ever in church and community affairs, which I felt were part of the same ministry. The youth center in the parsonage had become much too small, so together with a group of friends, we invested in a plan to purchase the Old Armory building and an empty store in downtown Windsor. The armory building already had a huge slot-car racing track which had been installed by the former owner, who also had operated a printing business there. Howard Carr joined in the effort, along with Bill Angliss, who

God's Call to Begin Things

was a longtime friend of my family and was a commercial pilot. We named the store "The Vermont Sports and Hobby Store" and we stocked it with all kinds of models, sports equipment, and the like. We even had a ski and boot section provided by Norm who had befriended me when he was a prisoner. Our store provided lots of services, including a commercial bus stop and we had a great variety of customers. J.D. Salinger, author of *Catcher in the Rye*, was one of them (although I don't recommend his book). He often shipped items on the bus that stopped at the store. He was known as a recluse but he did engage in limited conversation with us.

To replenish our supplies, I made the long trip to North Adams, MA, to select inventory from a huge warehouse. Our plan was not to make money for the investors but to pay for the extensive youth program and the armory building. It was a good plan, but just as it seemed we were getting going, Walmart and many other stores opened in West Lebanon, NH, a short drive from Windsor. So, our store died a slow death as did many other businesses in town. However, our youth program continued full blast. Almost all the children and teenagers in town were involved in some way. The Armory was a large brick building with hardwood flooring and we immediately installed basketball hoops and also purchased seventy-five sets of roller skates. So the building became a beehive of activity for the Windsor area youth as well as a men's basketball league. I was given an award as "Young Man of the Year" by the Rotary Club, something I treasure. But in all the activities, I tried to keep my ministry first and many heard the gospel as a result.

In the summer of 1965, the church rented Camp Good News in Charlestown, NH. This camp was located on an old farm and consisted of a large farmhouse, a barn converted into a meeting and dining room, plus some cabins. There was a swimming pool fed by a cold water brook, and some lawns for games. It was very highly organized with a specially written handbook for leaders. The objectives were clear-cut: Bible study, developing closer fellowship among the people, and of course, and the most important of all, making sure that all the campers were "born again" believers. When we began planning, we wondered how many people would actually sign up for the week, but when the time arrived, almost the entire church came along, plus some others— 105 full-time campers.

While the main purpose for camp was spiritual, we wanted everyone to have fun as well. We organized the entire group into two teams for competition consisting of points for Bible memory, games and sports, and for cabin care. The teams were "The Bread Baskets" and the "Horn Blowers." To accommodate the older folks, the farmhouse provided a nice refuge from all the continuous activities and accompanying noise. The house had nice rooms, a library, and most important on the cool late summer evenings, a fireplace.

The working staff consisted of me, Mike Hamblen, Mabel Hurd (our camp nurse), her son Norman, David Biebel, Bob Pomeroy, Gail Husted, Susan Bogart, and Amy Mason. Our speaker for the week was Rev. Paul Ferrin, a former pastor of our church and his wife, Erma, who also sang at the evening services. Part of each day was devoted to instruction, including swimming, archery with David as the instructor, and several other choices. The kitchen crew did a great job and Stuart Shepard provided the surprises with two bushels of sweet corn and boxes of delicious fresh strawberries grown on his farm.

As the week was winding down, several decisions for Christ had been made but the highlight of the whole week was the Friday night campfire. We had everyone form a huge circle around the fire and many gave testimonies. Some were about receiving Christ and others were about forgiveness and relationships. God had truly blessed our effort to please Him. As for me, I gave some very deep thought to the whole idea and reached the conclusion that in those five days, we as a church had accomplished as much, or more, than in the whole year round. Looking back, it was this great experience which led me down the path toward establishing Singing Hills. God would take care of that! Our church poet, Nettie Keay, had composed a poem about our family which was read at a post-camp party. It was entitled:

OUR BLESSINGS ON THE BIEBELS:

It doesn't seem quite possible
That five long years have passed
Since to the pulpit of this church
Our minister was asked,
He brought with him three young sons,
His wife and one small daughter
They're living at the parsonage
Like a parson's family oughter.

His wife's a very clever girl;
She cooks and sews and sings.
Her only vice is coffee break
And crispy onion rings.
Her children are such little scamps
They drive her off her rocker.
To get her "patients" back again
She's working for a doctor.

Now, Dave the tall and handsome one
Has gone to K.U.A.
We miss him at the old home base"
But he's not far away.
And Danny is the middle boy;
He's hardly ever still
But we can count on him most times
To win the Bible Drill.

Then Paul, "the quiet one," they say
Is clever with a pencil.
For he can draw a picture well
Without the aid of stencil.
At last on Biebel's family tree
The "Wee girl" blossom came;
A wiggly, giggly little lass,
And Judy is her name.

We've talked about the Biebel Boys,
The daughter and the mother.
We have so many things to say,
Let's talk about "The Other."
The "Other" one is Mr. "B"
The shepherd of our flock.
He's Chaplain of the prison too,
And works around the clock.

Now Mr. Biebel likes to boat,
And fish a stream or two.
With bow and arrow, or a gun
His hunting he will do.
There is a proverb that we know,
"to pass the buck is sin"
"Beak" leans on rocks in sweet repose
And lets the buck pass him.

In baseball, golf, or bowling games
There's no-one does much finer.
But hockey is the sport for him
In that he's quite a "shiner."
It looks to us like once a year
His wife has got him licked;

God's Call to Begin Things

> But in the pulpit Biebel stands
> And blames a hockey stick.
>
> Folks heckle him about his nose
> And his great appetite,
> We're throwing a big party now,
> So he'll get fed tonight
> P.S. With all the kidding laid aside;
> To get down to the letter
> We love you Biebels, one and all
> For where could we do better?

Sometime in 1967, I received a pleasant surprise! My friend, the warden of the Vermont State Prison, had recommended me for the Protestant chaplaincy of the Veterans' hospital in White River Junction, VT, and a time was set for my meeting with Mr. Foley, the personnel director. I explained to him what my mission there would be as I saw it, and even though he knew me to be an evangelical, he hired me. Perhaps my extensive community service suggested that I was more broadminded than some other conservatives.

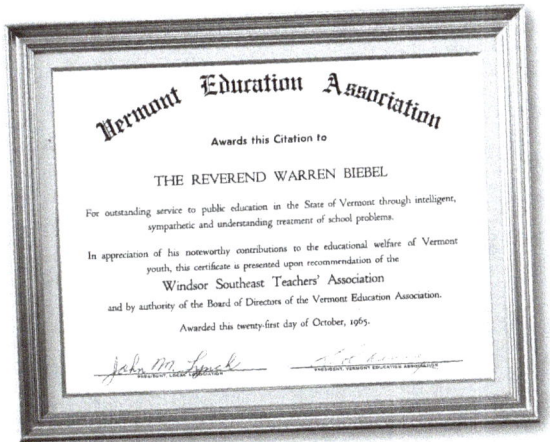

Even the Vermont Education Association was impressed enough with my volunteer work to present me with this certificate.

My résumé included the fact that I had received a special certificate for "outstanding service to the youth of my community" from a fairly "liberal" source, The Vermont Education Association.

This job not only opened a wonderful door for me to share the gospel with patients but provided a much-needed increase in our family income. So began thirteen years! My regular hours were sixteen each week plus being on call 24/7. I could be called whenever one of the patients was placed on the "Seriously Ill" list, meaning that the presiding doctor did not think the patient would survive. Over time, the emergency visit part of my job would lead to many deep experiences.

Leaving the prison chaplaincy produced several personal feelings. I had developed a respect on the part of some of the inmates, and I had enjoyed writing my stories in the "Green Mountain Graphic," newspaper. Ministering to the sick and sometimes dying patients would be much different from ministering to hardened and incarcerated men, but the goal would be the same, a life given to the Savior.

Toward the end of my prison chaplaincy, I had an invitation to speak at Goddard College in Plainfield, VT. The reason this was so unusual was that Goddard was among the most liberal colleges in the United States at the time and my evangelical belief and ministry was very well known. It didn't take long for me to get a taste of their culture when I passed several students at the entrance gate who were obviously "stoned." Since it was lunch time, I was ushered into the dining hall where I found the lunch to be okay, but it was being shared by dozens of dogs who wandered up and down and were getting parcels of food from the students. At the end of the meal, the college president came on with an appeal to the dog owners to control feces on the campus. Evidently that had become a problem for walkers. After lunch, I went to a room with about fifty students and answered questions about the prison and my chaplaincy. That was it for my visit but shortly after, it became national news that two girl students from Goddard had moved to Greenwich Village in New York City, a hotbed of radicalism. Both were killed when a bomb that they were making exploded. So, I wasn't surprised to see that this year, as I write this, for a commencement speaker, they had a former gang member and murderer for a featured speaker.

God's Call to Begin Things

In our family, things were happening too! Marian was working as a Medical Assistant to Dr. McCarthy in Claremont. David had gone to Kimball Union Academy, in Meriden, NH, on a full four-year scholarship and he made his mark there as editor of the student paper. However, he became disillusioned with the "herd" culture at the school and returned to Windsor to complete his high school education. One of his (and mine) highlights was for him to face Carlton Fisk who was from nearby Charlestown, NH, and was pitching in local high school games. Carlton later became a catcher for the Red Sox and was a hero in the 1975 World Series against the Cincinnati Reds when he hit his famous twelfth inning home run to extend the series to seven games. After he retired, he was elected to the Major League Baseball Hall of Fame.

Dan, Paul, and Judy were continuing their schooling. Dan was on the Windsor basketball team and scored lots of points. In 2012, he was elected to the "Wall of Fame" where his picture was hung on the wall of the beautiful new gymnasium at Windsor High School. Paul was involved in some sports but he continued to show signs of his interest in construction and electric trains. Meanwhile, Judy had grown to be a very pretty young woman and was excelling in academics and music. They all were involved in the youth work and each of them had special friends who frequented our home.

As for my personal interest, during the golf season, I played in the men's' twilight league as the member of a foursome. Our group did pretty well and each of us received a small trophy at the end of the season. I placed mine in a prominent position on the shelf in our TV room where we watched football. The Bible says, "Pride comes before a fall" and as I was sitting in my special chair on a Sunday afternoon, the trophy exploded with a bang! Lesson learned!

SINGING HILLS

As a pastor, I believed in using every possible means to win people to Christ and one of those was to have a series of Christian films on Sunday evenings during the Lenten season. It was the early spring of 1969, and the film for that evening was "I Beheld His Glory," the story of the Roman Centurion at the cross when he looked up at Jesus and exclaimed, "Surely this is the Son of God." This was a really moving film. At the service that night were Earl and Marian King from Meriden, NH. Earl was a member of the Meriden Baptist Church and was even the bell ringer and had pumped the bellows for the pipe organ in years past, but had never made a personal decision to receive Christ. That evening at the invitation, Earl came forward to make that decision and so began a wonderful story of real life.

At the time, there was no minister at the Meriden Baptist Church and I visited Earl and Marian several days later. In the course of our conversation, I was sharing my great interest in youth work and mentioned the family camp that our church had, but that those camp facilities would no longer be available. Earl responded to ask if such a camp could be built if the land was available and he invited me to take a walk with him around his property of 140 acres. It is very hard now to describe the land as it was then but it was typical land for a New England small dairy farm. The terrain was very hilly with no flat area that I could see and for the most part the land was covered by a mixture of large trees and brush. Earl took me to the top of a steep hill where he pointed out a pretty flat area which he said had at one time been a wheat field. There was a 360 degree view there including the hills and mountains of both New Hampshire and Vermont. There were a number of apple trees which we later learned were wild.

Earl and Marian King were wonderful folks, both in their later fifties. They were typical New England people, hard-working, honest, and very friendly. Earl had a collection of old farm equipment including a Ford dump truck, a John Deere bulldozer, several Ford tractors with cutting bars, and numerous other important machines. He also had a workshop in their basement where he always had something to fix. Each year Earl submitted and won a bid to do the roadside cutting in Vermont, which he did mostly by himself. When he said something, you knew he meant it, so his offer of the land to me set in motion another major change in my life and ministry.

Earl King (right) had some heavy equipment that he taught me to use.

For me and my family, it would mean leaving the successful ministry in Windsor, VT, and moving to Plainfield, NH. It would take extensive planning and a lot of faith! I personally was excited about the great possibilities of the property for a Christian Conference or retreat center, though the rest of the family were not so enamored with the idea. But I was certain that the Lord was moving in the whole thing as He had been in taking us first to Claremont and then to Windsor. The wisdom of those moves had been confirmed by their success.

The biggest question was: Where to begin? We knew that we would need a place to live and a master plan for the property. When I became sure that this was God's plan, I began to consider how I could leave behind all my activities in Windsor in a way that would ensure, as much as possible, the continued success of those church and community efforts. There were some things that were very obvious. The store had effectively been put out of business by the Mall opening in West Lebanon so it would have to be sold and the Old Armory Building turned over to the community. As for the church, I would continue to serve as pastor until I was assured that it would continue to prosper. In the meantime, our family would need to find a way to buy a separate parcel of land from Earl King where we could build a home. I turned the whole matter over to the Lord for wisdom and strength. Since my new ministry would be in proximity to the churches that I had served, I did all I could to assure the people that any retreat center to be built would not compete with former churches; rather it would contribute to the overall Christian ministry of the Twin State Valley (this is a term used to describe the Connecticut River Valley which divides New Hampshire and Vermont).

Our first house ultimately became the Director's home for Singing Hills.

Our first step was to purchase a plot of land from Earl on which to build our own home. The plot was 300 x 300 feet with a 100 foot strip down to Stage Road, a right of way that was required by the town zoning. The balance of the land had about 1,500 feet of frontage on Stage Road. Our choice for builder was Stowell Builders, who built a nice home for us at a reasonable price. Our son, Paul, was one of the crew and this was a precursor to what the Lord had in store for him in the future. The house included a kitchen, dining room, three bedrooms, and one bath. The basement area was unfinished at the time but was large enough for two more bedrooms, a bath, and a large recreation room, or even a second apartment. It was an exciting time for us to see our very first and very own house going up.

The next steps included preparing a Master Plan to present to the town officials for their approval. Documents had to be prepared and presented to the U.S. Government to obtain a 501(c)3 status as a non-profit Christian organization. A Board of Directors of five persons had to be chosen. All of this had to come together without any money. One of the great joys of my heart at the time was the support we received from the church members for a new venture and best wishes and prayers that were expressed at a "Going Away Party" that was given for us. A letter, which is copied here, was given to us to keep. Thank you church!

> "THE PEACE OF GOD, WHICH PASSETH ALL UNDERSTANDING, SHALL KEEP YOUR HEARTS AND MINDS THROUGH CHRIST JESUS"

Dear Pastor Biebel and Family;

It is with deep regret that we, as a Church must let our beloved Pastor and family leave our midst, and that we did not show this concern in a vocal response to the reading of your resignation as of the January 20th annual Business Meeting.

Pastor, you have given us many years of faithful service; even when you have been too ill sometimes to be at some of the services. You have faithfully brought to us a message of truth, challenge, hope and encouragement from the Word of God at all of our meetings; words of comfort and consolation to us as our loved ones have passed away; you have given a message of instruction and hope, and good wishes for our sons and daughters, brothers and sisters in Marriage Ceremonies; you have helped to lift up the spirits of those who have fallen or who have needed to be encouraged and brought into a closer walk with God.

Our whole town, as a matter of fact, is much indebted to you as you have, to the best of your ability, in what you felt was God's will for you, tried to get a good Youth Work started here, and there are many other services which you have rendered to make this town a better place to live in.

We owe much gratitude to your dear wife for her faithful service to our church in her ministry as our church organist, and in using her voice also in choir and solo work, holding office in the Women's group and on Music and Flower Committees. She used her hands to create some of the beautiful drapes that do so brighten up the downstairs rooms. She so graciously has allowed her home to be used for Sunday school classes, and has never made complaints about the preparation for such, or the clean up afterward.

We have enjoyed your sons and are proud of them and happy for them in the decisions they have made. We will miss them in the choir and in special things they do when they are able to be with us. And Judy, who has grown to be a very sweet little lady; we have enjoyed watching her grow too, and are happy she has been a part of our musical program.

All the Biebel family has had a hand in some of the janitor work also—even down to Judy helping to shovel walks. We pray that God will bless your children richly.

We know that you as a family, each in your own particular talents and services have looked for no glory in all these things. You have been humble and happy to do as unto the Lord.

We are sorry you will not be here with us, but happy for you as a family that God has given to you an opportunity to serve in a work which you have felt to be your calling, and that He has given a plot of land for this work and a home for you, and a little church that will be blessed by your ministry.

Thus, in this matter we must be willing to say, "Go in and possess the land the Lord has given you," and may His richest blessing be upon you and yours as you serve Him in the wonderful venture of faith.

> On behalf of our church family
> And in His Love,
>
> Nettie Keay, Church Clerk
> First Baptist Church
> Windsor, Vermont

God's Call to Begin Things

There was one other letter that I kept and treasured. It was from Ivis Scales, one of the older members of our church and one whom I had visited often at her home just off Route 44 at the base of Mt. Ascutney. Although most of my emphasis had been on young people, I brought the older people with me in that effort and they became a very important and enthusiastic part of it.

January 30, 1972

Dear Mr. And Mrs. Biebel;

I am not very good at saying things I feel, but I do want you to know I am so sorry you are leaving our church. I am so glad you will be near, and we will get to see you some times.

I always dread getting a new Pastor, maybe, because of past experiences. But anyway, it has been wonderful to have you this long, and I know the others you are going to, need you also.

And I am praying God will send us the right one to carry on the work here.

Ivis Scales

Love to you both,
Ivis

P.S. Was hoping, Marian, we could go to Gove Hill again this year. I am sure this car would make that hill. Wasn't so sure before.

While we were still living in Windsor and our house was being built in Meriden, my chaplaincy at the VA Hospital was continuing, and at the same time plans were consolidating for the property. A Board of

Directors consisting of five men was chosen. In selecting these five, my main consideration was not their financial standing but rather, their spiritual commitment. Meanwhile, after I had revised the "Statement of Purpose" to satisfy government requirements, we received our 501(c)3 status as a nonprofit Christian Corporation.

It was during the time of organization that one day Earl and I were working on the driveway entrance, that the Lord gave me the name for the property. I had been studying the book of Isaiah and memorizing Scripture. As I had been memorizing chapter 55, and as I looked around at the beauty of the surroundings, the Lord spoke clearly to me (not audibly) and said, "That's it!" That chapter begins with the wonderful invitation in the King James Version, "Ho, every one that thirsteth, come ye to the waters and he that hath no money, come, buy and eat."

The chapter goes on to tell the whole gospel story and results in the individual responding to God's Word and the result is, "You shall go out with joy and be led forth in peace. The mountains and hills shall break forth before you into singing and all the trees shall clap their hands. Instead of the thorns and weeds, fir trees and other fruitful trees shall flourish" (my paraphrase). This was a perfect description of what we prayed would happen to everyone coming onto this property. That had to be the name and it was "Singing Hills"! So Earl and I erected a large sign at the entrance to our driveway, "Welcome to Singing Hills."

This very large and heavy sign is still in place, welcoming one and all to Singing Hills.

Earl donated the property, but he did much more than that. He used his vehicles and machines to get things going on the property. For example, we knew that we would need to have a driveway for access to

God's Call to Begin Things

our new house and our first plan was to go straight up the hill, keeping it on the 100 foot strip right of way which our family had purchased from Earl. That required stripping the top soil and removing large rocks. Earl provided his John Deere bulldozer and dump truck to do the job. Earl's old Ford dump truck was in good working shape, except that in order to release the rear panel to drop the load, he had to reach out the driver's side window and pull a rope. One afternoon Earl drove in with a full load of gravel to spread on the new driveway. He proceeded up the hill to the spot, stopped, raised the truck body to dump the gravel and pulled the rope. The only thing was, the tailgate did not open and as the load shifted to the rear, Earl and the cab went straight up in the air. Enter Gordon Lapan, who became a regular at Singing Hills, as did his wife, Timmie. But on this day, he pulled the truck down with his machine and Earl was able to drop and spread the gravel. Earl was not the only one to have difficulty on that steep hill as we would find out in the winter to come.

Timmie Lapan was a faithful kitchen worker for many years.

Meanwhile, my ministry at the VA Hospital was continuing and included some difficult situations, but also some very humorous ones. I started out on the Respiratory Ward where I saw the devastating results of heavy smoking. Many of the patients were World War II veterans. It was sad to see the men struggling so hard to breathe. However, during the course of those thirteen years, I visited all the wards and met many patients. One of those was the cribbage champion of Vermont who wanted me play a game or two every time I came to his ward. Although I considered myself a pretty good player, I never won a single game!

Whenever the situation was right, I tried to bring some humor to and laughs into an otherwise drab environment. But there was sadness, too! There was a man who lived near Singing Hills who was a patient suffering from "Legionnaires' Disease," and was barely hanging on. I remember bending over and whispering that God loved him and that Jesus died for him. Shortly after that he died from the then mysterious disease that was later discovered to have something to do with the air conditioning.

As time went by, I met and became a friend of Maynard Young, a member of the administration. We had much in common and golf was an interest we both shared. The administrative staff occasionally had an afternoon off for a game of golf and on one particular occasion, we were playing at Crown Point Country Club in Springfield, VT. I was riding in a cart with Maynard and we were approaching the fifteenth tee where the foursome ahead of us was teeing off. As one of the group was getting ready to hit, Maynard said to me, "Don't get too close. He throws his club!" Sure enough, after dribbling a shot into a swampy area on the Par 3 hole, he wound up and threw his club into the area where it stuck in the mud.

On another occasion our round of golf turned into a spiritual experience. Maynard and I were playing at the Hanover Country Club and were coming toward the clubhouse on the seventeenth hole, with Maynard winning as he almost always did. We were approached by one of the clubhouse attendants who said that Maynard had a very important phone call. When he came back, Maynard had tears in his eyes. Helen, his wife, had called to tell him that she'd been diagnosed with breast cancer. I put my arm around my friend and had a prayer for Helen and I'm glad to say that she was cured after treatment.

Another friend at the VA Hospital was the Physical Therapist, Vic. He and I were assigned to make a trip to Washington, DC, for a conference of VA staff members. It was just before Christmas. Vic was a great guy, always with something funny to say. But he had an odd habit of saying, "Think you can handle it?" It was just a good natured expression. In Washington we were having lunch at a table with three psychiatrists. We were being served by waitresses who were African American and ours was a rather large lady. Vic had ordered tomato juice to go with the order, but as the waitress was turning to place the orders, he said, "Think you can handle it?" That was a bad mistake! When the orders were served, the waitress stumbled a bit and spilled the juice on Vic. The three psychiatrists thought that was great!

Heading home for Christmas, Vic and I boarded our Eastern Airlines jet and we were on our way. However, as we proceeded toward Logan airport, the weather deteriorated and we were heading into sleet and freezing rain. Looking out the window as we approached for landing, we could not see the ground and as it turned out, we were the last flight to land that winter night. Very scary! We were scheduled to make connection with a commuter flight, New England airways. That flight had been canceled along with the rest and we were told we would have bus transportation to White River Junction.

In the meantime, we met a young man I knew well from our youth programs, Robbie Bent. Robbie had arrived from the West where he was a college student, and had skis with him along with luggage. He had gone to the flight counter where he hoped to get a refund for his ticket but was informed that the airline had gone bankrupt and there could be no refund. He was broke! So Vic and I scraped together the ten dollars needed and he boarded the commercial bus with us. The ride home from Logan was no picnic either since the highways were slick and ice covered. But we all made it; surviving another memorable trip!

Back at the hospital, I was doing what I could to minister to those hurting. One such patient was Ted Bonneau. Ted was instrumental in helping us at Singing Hills. As an employee of the New Hampshire conservation division, his job was to assist landowners in planning and carrying out environmental projects. In our case, he got us a government contract to prune thirty acres of trees up fifteen feet from the ground. This was not an easy job but with persistence of Glen Stone and some others, we managed it. Later on, Ted would be the one to plan and oversee the construction of our large pond. He thus was not only a patient but also a friend. Ted was diabetic and had a very bad case, noticeable at first when he had trouble walking. Later his condition became so bad that he had to have amputations of both legs and finally the condition claimed his life there in the VA Hospital. I remember well how Ted accepted the inevitable with grace.

Ted Bonneau planned and oversaw the construction of our pond.

At the VA Hospital, I was often invited to speak at the AA meeting where I stressed that the "Higher Power," which they knew they needed and was part of their belief, was really Jesus! On one occasion a patient approached me to tell how he had actually been declared dead but was revived. He said that during his "death" experience he had a very pleasant sensation of warmth and light, which I had not heard anyone describe before, so I wasn't sure how to respond. I knew that the apostle Paul described his own near death experience in the New Testament, during which he was transported to the "third heaven" where he heard things that he was not allowed to tell. In the years following that patient's account, a number of books were published on the subject of "near death" experiences. Since there's such a variety of experiences, and some have admitted to making up their stories, I think the "jury" is still out on what this phenomenon is. I would say that if someone has one of these experiences, and it points them to Christ or deepens the faith that they already have in Him, then it was a good thing for them. But I would also suggest that, like the apostle Paul, they simply use that experience to bolster their faith, and not try to describe the details of what they saw or heard to others.

While our house was being completed, we went to work on the initial outdoor projects. One of the first was to plant several hundred spruce seedlings obtained from a program at the University of New Hampshire. I enlisted the help of the teenagers and all the trees were planted, scattered about the property. A second group would be planted later. The original driveway was partially abandoned and a new route established. However, that also had to be changed later because of water problems. We were planning a sports field and that involved some major bulldozing, leveling, and planting. Don Macleay, a local contractor, bulldozed the field and it became a great place for a variety of sports including softball, soccer, and many other games and activities.

Now came the real challenge—our first building. You can't have a conference center without having a Lodge, but where would it be and how could we fund its construction? One day, after our home had been completed, I was sitting in the living room looking out the picture window across the beautiful landscape, I noticed a flat area on top of a hill across the valley. This spot had been obscured by a stand of hardwoods, big pines, and brush. Without doubt, this had to be the spot for our main buildings!

Much of the lumber could come from the huge pines that would have to be removed. I had some experience with this from Claremont, where we had cut the trees and created the lumber from them to build the church. But cutting those huge pines was a project in itself. The roots had to be removed and that's where Earl came to the rescue again. I helped him, but not without some trepidation. The process involved partially exposing the roots, placing dynamite in the hole underneath, and laying a wire to a sheltered spot about 150 feet away. Then Earl would push the plunger on the igniter and, "BOOM," the stump would lift out of the ground and leave a big hole. This had to be done a number of times to ready the area for construction of the Lodge.

The first parts of the main lodge were constructed using lumber from our own property.

Another preliminary project was to put in a circular driveway around the top of the hill to give access to construction equipment. I had sketched plans for the original building, including dimensions. Once again, I was an unqualified architect but history proved that the building with all its faults was just what we needed to get started. That is when the hard work actually began!

Lumber had been cut and delivered back to our location, excavation was done, and the cement foundation had been laid. Singing Hills Lodge was underway!

Another thing that we absolutely needed was a dependable water supply. Don Allen, who was a Christian, had attended some of our programs and owned an artesian well drilling rig. It was mounted on the back of a truck and once a prospective site was decided upon, he would assemble the necessary piping and submersible pump, and other essentials and begin the process. Over a period of time, Don actually put in four artesian wells for us. One of them is located below the playground and has faithfully provided excellent water for the Lodge. Another well

God's Call to Begin Things

serves the original house, a third supplies the Pondview House and Hillside House, and a fourth had to be added when the Chapel-Family Center was built. That one required a depth of 400 feet and did not produce large volumes. The well at the Pondview location was only seventy-five feet deep and produced the most water of all. Another artesian well would be added later to service the Hilltop camping area.

We are so thankful to Don Allen, who would not accept any money for the projects! Don still sends contributions to Singing Hills. What a Christian and friend! Wish we had more like him!

We applied for a bank mortgage with the Mascoma Savings Bank and subsequently a group of bankers came up to survey the property. They took a good look around and approved our loan application, but I overheard one of the bankers say, "They can have the loan, but I don't believe they'll ever get the project done." They didn't take into consideration some of the great volunteers and workers, like Bill and Alice Jordan, Sandy Austin, Earl King, Wayne Purnell, Glenn Stone, Herb Bean, Sue Jones, Pastor Earl Lehman, Gordon and Timmie Lapan, and many more.

Of all the great staff and volunteer workers that participated in the success of Singing Hills, the most important were Dave and Josie Lersch who came to us after retiring from IBM. If there is someone somewhere who knows everything, that has to be Dave. He is a whiz with electronics and computers, a master plumber, a flooring expert, and lots more. When you put him in combination with Scott

Dave and Josie Lersch were among the most indispensable volunteers who ever served at Singing Hills.

Walker, you've got winners. What an asset and blessing it was to have them on our staff and to have the equipment building constructed where Dave could have an office and various machines and tools kept under cover. These men had a hand in just about every project and repair job that was required. In the meantime, Josie joined Timmie Lapan to do one of the most important jobs of all—cooking.

After Marian and I retired, these folks continued on for many years and actually, Dave is continuing to help on a shortened schedule, even now. It was nice to have Dave and Josie drop in at our home in Florida while on their annual winter "camper" trip. Dave was continuing to volunteer at the Life for Youth Ranch in Vero Beach during the northern cold winter months.

We had not just been waiting idly for the day when we could have overnight guests. Singing Hills was already hosting many guests. We had a huge tent where we held spaghetti dinners and cookouts. The Town of Plainfield recreation program for young children was using our property. We had built, with the planning of Ten Bonneau, a beautiful pond to replace an original smaller one. After we received the necessary State of NH permits Don Macleay brought in a huge bulldozer and excavation began. We chose the new pond location because I had discovered springs and even some running water in the selected area. In size, the pond was about 300 feet across from every perspective around the shoreline. The dam was about thirty feet across the top and six feet above the water line with a spillway in case of flooding. It had to be planted with grass,

Don Macleay excavated and completed our beautiful swimming and skating pond.

but could not have trees or bushes with deep roots. It would be sixteen feet deep at the lowest point, with sloping sides to the edge. The material removed was used for the large dam. Fed by spring water, it is a beautiful pond for swimming and wildlife. Trout were added later and in the wintertime it made a great place for ice skating.

Our family life was continuing and each of our teenagers were pursuing interests of their own as well as sharing family times. The summers continued to include time at our cottage at Baptist Pond where a small outboard and a sailboat provided lots of fun together as well as the good fishing. The family now included two dogs, Candy and Cyrus. These dogs got along really well but mirrored each other's behavior. When they were good they both were good but when they were bad, they were bad! On one occasion they spotted a chipmunk in a stone wall and both took off and before I could intervene they had killed the little animal. Then there were the run-ins with skunks and the unsuccessful baths in tomato juice. But the most memorable occasion happened when they simultaneously attacked a porcupine and came away with mouths and noses full of quills. After a hurried trip to Fletcher's Veterinary clinic, they were anesthetized and the quills removed. The ride home was quite interesting with two dogs that looked like they had been out for a night on the town. These were the experiences of living in the country. We also had a cat called "Smudge" because of what looked like a smudge of soot on her white nose. Otherwise, she was black. Unfortunately one night she went out for her regular rounds and never came back, probably a victim of a fisher cat or coyote.

We were anxious to see our ministry opportunities grow and had a large teenage program. Many of those continued on in the Christian life and some are in the Lord's work today, including Harold Jones, our current pastor, Brig Judy, a missionary to the Indians in Manitoba, Canada, Bob Pomeroy, a pastor and his wife a nurse who volunteers on mission trips. Glenn Stone, one of our first workers, became a pastor and still is. Early in his time with us, "Rocky," as we called him, was sleeping in a small cabin near our first pond. The previous day we had been clearing brush and burning it. Marian and I were fast asleep in our bedroom at home when there came an excited knock on our door! "Mr. Biebel, there's a fire in the tree," Rocky exclaimed. I hurriedly got up, called the fire department (Marian says that I brushed my teeth first), and headed to the pond area. Sure enough, there was a huge old tree trunk that was hollow, and flames were shooting out the top like a volcano. It was determined by the Fire Chief that sparks from our fire the day before had gone down the hollow trunk and ignited the stubble that had gathered in there.

There was another incident at that first pond. It was there that we had ice skating for the teenagers and that necessitated clearing the snow, so one morning I took the snow shovel, jumped into the black Ford truck and Cyrus, our dog, who went everywhere with me, jumped in on the passenger side. Cyrus, a real character of a dog (an English Springer Spaniel) had a way of expressing his likes and dislikes and when I wouldn't let him out to play in the snow, it was clear that he wasn't happy. After I finished clearing an area on the ice for skating, I returned to the truck, looking forward

"Cyrus" was my constant companion for years as Singing Hills developed.

to getting warm on the frigid day. I arrived at the truck to find that Cyrus had locked both doors by jumping on them and pushing the locking levers down. That meant a walk, for me, back to the house through the snow, and then back to the truck with the extra key. He had been a bad dog but I forgave him.

The years from 1972 to 1976 were devoted almost entirely to completing the first stages of the lodge building, with the kitchen, dining-living room, and two guest wings. We were, in effect, acting as our own contractors and the volunteers who had expertise in certain areas were vitally important. I was trying to do things that were completely foreign to me. Herb Bean came to our rescue in the installation of six circulators for the heating zones but I helped and did a lot of soldering of copper pipes. The Queneau family, who attended the Meriden Church at the time, graciously donated a "Tarm" furnace that was made in Denmark and which burned both oil and wood. Sandy Austin was a sort of construction boss and soon the framing was done and walls, floors, and ceilings began to appear. Much of the material was pine wood from our own trees. Over the years, many changes had to be made to meet the fire codes.

July 4, 1976 was a very special date for our country and for Singing Hills. We all had worked into the night of July 3 to finish painting the ceilings and touching up. The big stone fireplace, which had been built with fieldstone from the property and constructed by Pastor Earl Lehman of Grace Baptist Church in Milford, CT, was beautiful and provided a warm welcome. To say that the building was finished would be an exaggeration. That night, it consisted of a living room, three bedrooms in the north wing and one bath, which had an old fashioned bath tub. For our first guests, two ladies from Windsor hazarded an overnight—Ivis Scales and Edna Beaulmont. How I thank the Lord for these two adventurers who helped to launch us on our way. What a great way to celebrate the two hundredth anniversary of our country. We had a dinner and concert that was open to the public. The dining tables had to be folded up and the chairs set out for the audience of about forty people to enjoy the evening.

From the very start it was evident that the Lord was blessing and leading at Singing Hills. He brought us groups for retreats, dedicated staff members, and special people, in those early days, who believed in our mission. Although we had a tiny, ill-equipped kitchen, we had cooks who always turned out great meals. Marian helped and Alice Jordan, Timmie Lapan, and Mikel Wells, along with other volunteers, got us off to a great start.

As we were moving forward with the development of Singing Hills, one of the important people helping to make it a success was Dave Biebel, our son. Dave became Associate Director in 1981, and it was his vision and expertise that put a much-needed charge into the growth. Programs that he initiated and helped to carry out included: "Music in the Mountains," which was very successful annually, on Labor Day weekend for a number of years. It attracted hundreds of people to enjoy numerous music groups who entertained outdoors under a big tent for an all-day program. Another program that Dave initiated was the Friendship Golf Tournament, which was held in spring and fall at a variety of area golf courses. This event attracted a sizable group of men and women who became regulars with their families at Singing Hills. In some cases, their involvement even led to others who not only came to Singing Hills themselves but participated in volunteer work. Having Dave with us for six years was a great encouragement, with many new guests and groups using our facilities year-round by the time he was called to a specialized ministry to Christian doctors and medical and dental students in the Northeast.

Our family involvement not only included Dave. Dan did some

amazing work in constructing huge stone walls and clearing land to make a beautiful site for our top-of-the-hill camping area which is so popular with groups that they often return time after time. And it can honestly be said that without Paul, Singing Hills would not have the beautiful buildings that comprise it today. Everything that he and his crews have done and are still doing is special. The woodworking in the main Chapel, the pulpit in the King Memorial Chapel and the wood designs, not only honor my Mom and Dad and Earl and Marian King, but more importantly they honor the Lord.

Dedication of the cross in the newly finished "King Chapel"

Of course, there's another one of our family, Judy, who is and has been the "First Lady" of Singing Hills. Her demanding job is to plan and carry out special retreats, do extensive office work, which includes the production of advertising and fund-raising material. She also stepped in, for several months, when there was a need for a cook in the kitchen. And we are eternally grateful that Judy and the Lord combined to bring Singing Hills its great Director, Don Jordan. He has completed many years of guiding and leading Singing Hills through "thick and thin" and has made it what it is today, led by God's hand.

As a result of the golf tournaments, the Helgerson family came from Rhode Island and all the men and women were golfers. We had tournaments at Crown Point Country Club in Springfield, VT, and others at the Country Club of New Hampshire and at Eastman Estates in Grantham, NH. We had great times and awarded prizes to the winners. One of the side benefits of these was not only their continuing participation but we were able to purchase at a very small price a Ford 440 tractor with a loader and backhoe from Paul Helgerson, who was a general contractor.

That machine was used to terrace the tubing hill and to dig a wildlife pond in the valley at the top of the hill that later became our camping area. I also used the Ford 440 to build five miles of trails up and around the hills. That required tearing up roots and leveling ground. Anyone using the trails today must wonder how this was done and I can't answer that. I guess I just started at the beginning and stopped when it was all done. The trails wend their way through beautiful stands of hardwoods, pines, and thick hemlock patches. The woods are populated by deer, wild turkeys, bobcats, coyotes, an occasional bear, and rarely, a wild boar.

One of the most unusual finds happened when Ron Brown and I were walking the trails and in a muddy patch, there were the tracks of a large cat. We returned to the house, took some Plaster of Paris and returned to the spot where we made a cast of the very clear print. We were sure it was a print of a mountain lion and since New Hampshire denied that mountain lions existed in the state, we called the Fish and Game Department and a wildlife expert came to see the print. He agreed with our assessment, but asked if he could take the cast to the University of New Hampshire to be analyzed. He promised to return it to us but we never heard about it again.

During the late 1970s and early 1980s, progress continued on the lodge building and a large addition was added that would include a large dining area with dormitory rooms in the basement underneath. Larger groups were beginning to come and on one occasion a group from St. Paul's Episcopal Church in Greenwich, CT, made reservations for a winter retreat. In the meantime a single gentleman, a widower, came to stay and melded into our staff. Horace Evans would be with us for quite a long time, housed in one of our available rooms. He was very helpful in keeping the wood fires going, day and night. As the large group from Greenwich arrived, we were not totally ready. The basement area under the dining room was not complete and the walls had to be divided with hanging blankets for the girls' dorm. That weekend turned out to be one of the coldest ever, but the teenagers had a great time tubing downhill and ice skating. They had come on a commercial bus and the driver, named Paul, stayed for the entire time. I had opportunity to share the gospel with him.

When Sunday morning came, the temperature had dropped to well below zero and the weather forecast was warning of a "Northeaster" coming up the coast. Paul, the driver, was anxious to get the group organized and going; however, no matter what we did, the bus would not start. We had every possible warming device in place to get the motor going, all to no avail. I'll never forget what happened next! I said to Horace and Paul and several others, "You pray about this and let *me* try." They were praying at the front of the bus when I got into the driver's seat, turned the key and the motor started on the first attempt. Was that a coincidence? I don't think so. But this whole event was typical of challenges we faced in those early days of development and which have continued until now.

One of those challenges that I personally faced was to keep myself in tip top physical shape and one thing I did was to jog around and up and down the driveway every night. One evening as I was jogging, I experienced a sudden and very sharp pain in my abdomen. I barely made it back to the house and Marian hurriedly drove me to the Valley Regional Hospital in Claremont, NH, where I was admitted. I found myself in the ICU ward, initially diagnosed with a heart attack. After five days, the pain hadn't subsided, in fact it was worse! The decision was made to call in a surgical specialist from Windsor, VT, and within five minutes of examining me, they prepared me for gallbladder surgery which revealed gangrene in the gall bladder, a life threatening condition, had it burst. In those days, this type of surgery required a sizable incision in the abdomen and I still have a twelve inch scar as a memento of a very narrow escape.

The next few years were marked by the comings and goings of staff families, including the Lohmans, the Robtoys, the Holdens, and later the Strouts. A number of individuals also served as staff members, including local teenagers and college students. Bob and Ellen Oberkotter were great friends and their girls, especially, became staples of our staff as did the Drye family. Summer employment was provided for most of our own grandchildren and some of the youth in the town.

Dave and I were providing some pastoral encouragement to a lady from Springfield, VT, Ruth Stone. Ruth was a widow who had come to events that had been held at the lodge. She lived with her elderly mother, which sometimes made Ruth's life difficult. One of us spoke with Ruth whenever she needed to talk. We had noticed a slight problem that she had with concentrating and also with her balance. A letter that she wrote to us in early 1978 tells what happened:

WHAT HAS SINGING HILLS MEANT TO ME?

Words cannot express my very deep feelings and great appreciation for this fine Christian community. Singing Hills was introduced to me by a saintly woman, Mabel Hurd, who had been very close to the Biebel family for many years. This was in 1977 shortly after my first husband died with lung cancer. I was devastated at this time and started coming to Singing Hills to contact Warren to request Christian counseling. At that time there was just the lodge and the two buildings where Warren and David

God's Call to Begin Things

lived. I continued to receive great religious help and spent much time here and the Lord granted me spiritual healing in body, mind and spirit. Here in this place, I came to really know my Lord. I became a "born again Christian."

In January of 1984 Warren and I committed and dedicated the coming year to the Lord. A few weeks later I was diagnosed with a brain tumor, requiring surgery. The Singing Hills staff and the whole Biebel family supported me and gave me the courage and help to face this coming ordeal. I spent two full weeks in Dartmouth Hitchcock Hospital and not one day passed that someone did not come from Singing Hills to see me. My complete recovery was a miracle and I give God all the glory. On August 28th I was introduced to the man who has now been my husband for nearly fifteen years and I acquired a family of two children, three grandchildren and a brother and sister-in-law. During these fifteen years there have been time of serious illnesses, including Frank's two bouts with cancer but Singing Hills has always been a source of strength and courage for me and will always have a very special place in my heart. When things get tough, I close my eyes and think of the peace and contentment that I found there. It is with much regret that I am unable to attend at least a day of the 25th Anniversary weekend but my mother is very ill. It is such an important ministry to be carried on and all to the glory of God! May God continue to bless it and all those who come there.

Ruth Stone Belden was a special friend of Singing Hills.

In Christian Love,
Ruth Stone Belden

Many momentous things were about to happen within our family. It was quite obvious when we visited my Mom and Dad at 235 Raven Terrace in Stratford, CT, that their ability to maintain the house and property was diminishing. Maintenance was a problem and Dad did most of whatever got done. Mom was ten years older than Dad and had a severe long-term thyroid problem. They did, however try to do things for pleasure, such as afternoon trips to the Trumbull Mall for ice cream and enjoying their nineteen inch TV, which provided entertainment. However, it became increasingly evident that the time was approaching when they would need assistance. This was confirmed when Mom had several falls and on one occasion had to be hospitalized and then transferred to a nursing home for personal care. So we were thinking that soon they would need to be with us. Dad resisted the idea for a period of time, until he realized the potential cost of the nursing home.

My father, Warren, Sr., and my mother, Mary on the occasion of their 50th wedding anniversary

A new wing was added to our house with one large room with a small bath that would meet their need for a bedroom and sitting room but would open into the dining room and living area of David and Ann and family. It also had a spiral staircase up to our bedroom above them. This meant there were four generations living together in one house.

God's Call to Begin Things

Our time at Singing Hills was a daily adventure filled with high-mountain and deep-valley experiences. It was thrilling to see how God kept us moving forward, always building, always intent on winning souls to Christ and nurturing them in the Christian life, and always with no money in the bank. Although Marian was doing a variety of jobs in addition to her secular work, neither of us took a salary from Singing Hills for the first eight years. Our income came from my chaplaincy, a small amount from the Meriden Church, and Marian's income as a Medical Assistant. Somehow, we were able to pay our small staff with money that was beginning to dribble in from groups and donors. In the beginning we had what we called the "101 Club," which would be comprised of 100 folks who would pledge $1.00 per week, along with Earl King who had donated the property. Several kept their donations coming for years. One elderly lady raised her pledge to $200.00 per month for ten years, until her death. She had a great vision for the ministry and when we had Sunday morning services for the staff and any in the community who wanted to join with us, she brought along her mandolin and played along with the piano for the singing. God bless you, Clarice Geer! Actually, she sort of adopted Marian as her daughter and made contributions to her doll collection. She loved to have Marian come to her home and they would make music together with the piano and mandolin. They wrote a couple of songs together. She missed us very much when we moved away but made telephone contact once a week, just to talk.

Clarice Geer was one of our most faithful supporters.

At Singing Hills I was still pondering what direction we would be going. For the first few years I thought that we should sponsor many of the retreats and activities, ourselves. For a short time, I held Sunday services but began to feel that wasn't the direction the Lord was taking us so I encouraged those who had been coming to get involved in the good churches available in our area, and I became interim pastor at the Meriden Baptist church for six years. The Lord blessed there, too, and at the end I was able to recommend Harold Jones, one of our own "teenagers," as pastor to succeed me at Meriden Baptist, which he did and where he still serves as I write this. Actually he is now my pastor.

There are some events and special people who stand out in my mind:

Dr. Bill Krause, a general surgeon, was an exceptional man. His home base was the Windsor Hospital where he, Dr. Ballantine, and Dr. Waterman provided excellent medical care. Dr. Krause took a special interest in Singing Hills and my work with the youth. On one occasion he invited me to go fly fishing at a private fishing club where he was a member. He tried his best to teach me the special art of casting an artificial fly out with the rod and landing it in the right spot. But it was not to be; I never got away from my preference for live bait. But the occasion with Dr. Krause that was burned into my memory was one day when he and I were driving from Windsor, VT, to Singing Hills in Plainfield, NH. We had just crossed the Connecticut River through the covered bridge and were heading north on Route 12A when we saw a small open red roadster sports car stopped in a strange angle in the middle of the road. There were two pretty young girls sitting upright in the open convertible—both were dead! Obviously the car had rolled a number of times and both had broken necks. Dr. Krause and I were the first on the tragic scene and he did a hasty examination of the girls only to find that nothing could be done. He was a very sensitive man and deeply saddened by that event.

In 1975, David had been called to be an assistant pastor with Joe Bubar in Muskego, Wisconsin but in 1976 Joe passed away. In 1978 Dave was called to pastor an Evangelical Free church in Carney, Michigan, in the Upper Peninsula. Marian and I, and Dad and Mom Miller were able to visit on the occasion of David's ordination about a year later. We made the trip together, by car. As we were returning along what was called the "Queen's Highway" in Canada, we passed through Toronto. I was driving Dad Miller's Buick when I heard a siren and was soon pulled over by a Canadian officer. He asked for my license and when he saw the "Rev." part he said, "Reverend, you were exceeding the speed limit." I offered a pathetic excuse, saying I was going with the flow of traffic and his response was, "You, of all people should know that following the crowd is not right!" Thankfully, he didn't give me a ticket.

Twenty Great Years of Blessing with a Touch of Sorrow

Harry and Joann Dopson and their daughter Sheri, who was confined to a wheelchair, became good friends and supporters of the ministry of Singing Hills. They arranged a large group of ladies to come from their church in Manchester, NH, for a retreat. It was in October of 1978 and I was especially honored to be their speaker. There was one special moment when in the final testimony time, many of the ladies spoke of how they had overcome unhappy childhood experiences with family members.

Joann, Harry and Sheri Dopson were frequent guests at Singing Hills.

Just as we were closing, Marian came out of the kitchen with tears in her eyes and crying, "Jonathan (our almost four-year-old grandson) is sick and in a coma," she said. We went from the mountain peak to the deepest valley, in a moment of time. Herb and Edi Hutchinson had become regular singers and group song leaders

Edi and Herb Hutchinson provided many hours of inspirational music.

and Edi had a special song called, "Lord, you light up my life," which had been introduced nationally by Debbie Boone. Edi had changed a few words to make it a song to the Lord. She sang it especially for me at that time and it has been special every time we get together. I even called her one day and she sang it for me over the phone.

For the next few weeks, my family and I and our friends all over the country prayed for Jonathan, who was in the Milwaukee Children's Hospital. I tried to do my outdoor work, but found myself praying often, beside a log or tree. But our plan was not God's and He took Jonathan to be with Him that October, 1978. It was then that I did some real deep searching of Scripture. I felt that the most important answers would come from Jesus, Himself and I found deep comfort in His words concerning little children. He spoke of their value in God's sight; "Except you become as a little child you cannot enter God's kingdom" and "in heaven their angels do always behold the heavenly Father." This brought me special comfort, and confidence I would see Jonathan again.

I showed Jonathan how to drive a lawnmower.

Singing and music were becoming more prevalent in our own sponsored programs and we had some excellent groups and soloists, Phil Lunati had a beautiful voice and had actually sung in a quartet with Elvis Presley before Elvis went into rock and roll. He had cut a number of excellent tapes. Ken and Martha Pilkenton were from Texas and their music had a touch of Texas in it. Martha had a movie star appearance, but she loved fishing for horn pout. (like a little catfish). She went fishing one day at a small pond along route 12A and did catch some "pouts." The LaChance family was extremely talented and they all participated in several concerts that we had at the lodge. One summer during Jimmy Carter's presidency there was a gas shortage and no one was traveling. We had scheduled the LaChances for the weekend and they had come from Rhode Island, themselves, but there was no audience to hear them. So, we had just enough gasoline to go fishing in the White River in Vermont. While going north on route 12A and the Interstate toward Royalton, VT, we didn't pass a single car. Fortunately, the gas shortage was short-lived and somehow Singing Hills survived the drought.

When I think back today about those twenty years that God gave us at Singing Hills, two things stand out in my memory. First, there were the great people and second, there were the constant ongoing projects. An example of a person who was not one of the most prominent people, but who made a small contribution while with us was one employee who came to us straight from city life and was quite naïve about country life. He even thought that cows just gave milk when they wanted to—like having spigots. As for fishing, he never had touched a rod. I was interested in helping him to expand his limited life and decided to take him fishing to the White River. Along the river in South Royalton there is a parking area right next to a deep, swirling eddy, a great looking spot to cast a line. The only thing is the number of fishermen and women stopping there to fish was high because the spot was so easy to reach. But this would be a great place to teach someone who had never been fishing before. After a few practice casts, he awkwardly tossed his line into the swirl. Wow! Something big hit it! So that is how the city boy got his first fish; a four-pound walleye.

Back at Singing Hills, we were stocking our own pond with brook trout and rainbow trout purchased from a local trout farmer, who had a hatchery just off Stage Road in Plainfield. Our fish prospered in the spring-fed pond and we enjoyed feeding them from our small dock. They would come in a frenzy to be fed, as soon as they saw us or even our shadow, and after two years we had some trout that were two pounds or more. Then one year there came a summer drought that found a lot of large dead trout floating on the surface, lacking sufficient oxygen. Only the small, newly hatched trout survived.

Chip Brown and the beautiful entrance sign he made

One family that helped us in a big way was the Brown family - Clint, Charlotte and Chip, their son. Clint always seemed to be there when we needed someone to rake leaves and Chip designed, built, and erected the entrance sign that still graces the entrance on Stage Road.

An exciting sidelight to this was that Chip fell in love with another volunteer who actually came from a church not far from his own in Connecticut. They both had children from former marriages and a lot of doubts and issues to overcome. In one of the most unusual weddings ever held, Chip Brown and Marian Hansen were married by me, without any fanfare, fancy dress, or even permanent rings, in front of the big stone fireplace in the living room of Singing Hills Lodge. They had waited until the very last day that their license would lapse. The witnesses were two guests (ladies from Montreal), plus our dog, Cyrus (just for fun). Actually, several love relationships, weddings, and even funerals have been part of this ministry.

Clint and Charlotte were kind enough to invite us to take a much needed vacation at their condominium on Marco Island on Florida's west coast. All we had to do was to get there. We took them up on their offer, and drove all the way. We enjoyed our week there although our apartment was located in the center of town and the shoreline was almost completely built up with tall buildings. In order to get to the open beaches we had to walk through a narrow path. Once we were on the beach we were visited by numerous sales persons offering free gifts if we would come to hear a discussion on, "Why we should buy a timeshare." Later, the Browns bought another condominium in Vero Beach, FL, on the Atlantic Coast, located on a small river that wended its way through a golf course located behind the building. They made us the same offer to use it, as the one at Marco Island, for a vacation. We were impressed with the location and it would become a stepping stone toward our eventual retirement and the continuing saga of our lives. Marian and I both loved the fishing village environment of the area, the ocean views and beaches. Actually, it would be difficult not to like it.

Another couple that came to us and became interested in helping was Wayne and Betty Purnell. Wayne was a veteran of World War II and had been a paratrooper. It was during the Battle of the Bulge that Wayne, with thousands of other paratroopers, landed either among the enemy or behind enemy lines. Many were captured or killed. For Wayne, it was behind the lines and the experience left him fearful, psychologically. I had the privilege of encouraging him on many occasions. He was also a master plumber with a specialty in installing and correcting heating systems. The Lord knew that we needed his expertise because we were experiencing a slight deficiency in the heating system that I had a big part in installing. Herb Bean had installed the six circulators correctly and I had done much of the soldering of what seemed

Bette and Wayne Purnell became our very good friends.

to be endless copper pipes. It didn't take long for Wayne to find the problem. I had put in all the heat directional valves backwards and they were only permitting a diminished flow of hot water. Oh, well, the problem was soon corrected!

We became very friendly with Wayne and Betty. They would often come to volunteer for a week at a time. Betty helped in the kitchen while Wayne did his "thing," which there was no end to. We wanted to do something nice for them in return. We asked Charlotte and Clint Brown if Wayne and Betty could share our time at the condo in Vero Beach, Florida, the next time we went and they agreed. Well, it seems that the river banks attracted alligators to sun themselves and some were being fed by well-meaning folks who didn't recognize the danger in doing so. On one particular day the lady next door went out to feed the alligator, that was very close to our door, too, and she slipped and fell on the bank and the gator started toward her. It was Wayne's turn to be a hero again as he rushed out and pulled the grateful woman to safety.

While our main interest was still in Singing Hills, we could sense that our work there might be nearing an end. After eighteen years of hard work and experiences that required an all-out effort, physically, mentally, and spiritually, we were like a piece of favorite clothing, not ready to be put in storage. We were still intact but feeling a little shopworn. Eight years of pastoring in Claremont, thirteen in Windsor, thirteen overlapping at the VA Hospital, with six years at the Vermont State Prison and six in Meriden plus twenty in building Singing Hills—the wear was showing. Our close-knit family was feeling it, too, with both blessings and heartaches. Marian's Mom had gone out to sweep the sidewalk on August 30, 1980, and suffered a fatal heart attack; so she left us to be with the Lord. Dad Miller was lonely and thus married a long-time widow and friend, Eleanor Lowndes in March 1981. They had one and a half years of happiness prior to his death October 22, 1982.

One of the bright lights for them was the purchase of one of our cottages on Baptist Pond and the enjoyment they had there. "Gramp" Miller especially liked taking the small outboard out to the island in the center of the pond. A good day for him was catching a bass and a bad day was dropping his rod overboard. We were happy that they could have those hazy, lazy days of summer at the cottage.

In 1984 and 1985 big things were happening at Singing Hills. Our original home had been purchased by Dave and Ann [it would later become property of Singing Hills] and a new house, called

My Mom and Dad loved their time at Hillside House.

the Hillside House, was designed by Marian and Paul with two apartments connected by a kitchen in between. My Mom and Dad had their own side with living room, bedroom, and bath. They shared the kitchen with us and we had our own apartment on the other side. The house would see an expansion in the future, as every other building has, to become staff housing and a place for small retreats of up to twenty people in the downstairs area.

Something happened, that at the time seemed insignificant, but turned out to be really important. Bill and Alice Jordan were both working on our staff and one of their two sons, Don, was graduating from Kimball Union Academy and he too became a staff member, doing a variety of jobs, for the summer. Then he went on to Keene State College. Our daughter, Judy, was graduating from Lebanon High school, a very pretty member of the family. Our boys, too, were growing handsome and entering the "search" stage of life to select the nicest and the best looking girls. For Don, the search started and ended with Judy, but there was something else. Don had a deepening love for the ministry of Singing Hills and it was only the Lord who knew that after marrying Judy and completing college at Keene State and an interim period of other jobs, he would be the one to succeed me as the "Captain" of Singing Hills. I use that term because taking the growing ministry through the years ahead would be like guiding a ship through icebergs and storms as well as calm seas.

Don and Judy Jordan took the helm of Singing Hills in 1990.

As the middle and late 1980s came, new buildings were built and we put them all to use. The Chapel–Family Center complex was our biggest project and Paul and his workers did a fabulous job of creating

Ken Roberts, a great carpenter, singer, and yodeler, died young but left his mark in many places including our Main Chapel.

a building that exuded warmth and welcome to all comers. A professional architect had designed the building, including the chapel with its open beams. He lived in Bridgeport, CT, and was associated with Black Rock Church and like others, had been to Singing Hills on a ski weekend and appreciated the ministry that we offered. One of the projects in the building was the fireplace and chimney built by professional stone masons and requiring about 1,000 field stones. All of these had to have at least one flat side and I well remember scouring all the old stone walls for the ones that qualified and lugging them to the staging area to keep the masons on schedule.

It reminded me of the time that Earl King and I had built the chimney of the lodge out of cement blocks. In order to do so, we had to first build scaffolding and then move the blocks higher and higher, leveling and mortaring them until we reached the top, forty feet high.

Paul put a great finishing touch on the main chapel with a large wooden cross surrounded by special wood cut and designed to meet at the cross itself. This same special design was repeated later in the Earl and Marian King chapel adjacent to the lodge dining room, with a stained glass window in the form of a cross, installed as the focal point. This is a memorial to my mother.

Five years later, Paul designed and constructed a beautiful pulpit of special imported wood in memory of my father, in front of the stained glass cross. Thank you Paul! For Dan, his "calling" seemed to be to improve and take care of the environmental needs of the property. In the course of time, he built huge stone walls, trimmed countless trees, and greatly improved the upper camping area.

Meanwhile on another of our Florida trips, God's timetable for us was moving forward. Once again, while staying in Clint and Charlotte's condo, we regularly went bike riding around the complex. Then, one day we decided to take a ride to Sebastian, a fishing town about twenty-five miles north on Route #1. Thanks to Chip Brown, we had access to his blue, Chevy convertible. We were on a scouting expedition, so I was driving very slowly as we perused the sights that were unfolding, Passing through the town of Wabasso, FL, I was going slowly, because we were looking for a real estate office. Evidently I was going too slowly, because a police officer pulled us over and wanted to know why I was driving like that. After we explained to him where we were from and what we were doing, he bid us go and wished us luck but said we should not go that slow. We continued on until we came to a large billboard that said; "Welcome to Sebastian—population 5000 people and 5 old grouches."

Heading into Sebastian, we came to the corner of Main Street and Route #1 where we saw a small building with a sign "Florida Realtors." Should we go in? What were we doing here anyway? We didn't have much money, but would be receiving a small pension soon and a small inheritance. So we thought it would be fun just to see some of the properties. The Realtor, in this case, was a pleasant man who took us all around Sebastian, looking at many homes. Some immediately took our eyes, especially one bordering on a small lake. It was a Cape Cod style, a two-story building with garage and nice landscaping. This dream came to a screeching halt when we learned the asking price. Moving on, we saw a number of nice homes; in fact Sebastian, itself, seemed to us to be a beautiful community.

There was one last home to view. It was located in a small development of fifty homes called "River's Edge." The home we looked at and immediately fell in love with was of masonry construction with a stucco facing. It had two bedrooms, two baths, living room, sitting room, dining room, kitchen, and the attached garage contained the laundry area with extra plumbing already installed. It had a lovely lot located on a cul-de-sac at the end of a street called Gail Road. One of the features of the property was that it included a one-fiftieth ownership of a recreation lot bordering on the Sebastian River, complete with a boat launching ramp and an opportunity for a small dock. The house was owned by an Army officer who no longer used it and his asking price was $65,000. As we drove back to Vero Beach, Marian and I had our separate thoughts. She was thinking about the negative aspects confronting

We loved our home in Sebastian, FL.

us if we were to purchase this property. There were the finances, the fact that we weren't quite at retirement yet, and how would we use and maintain it in the meantime? Back at Vista Royale we discussed the subject. We both loved the property but could we and should we do it? The outcome for us is what it always has been: Let the Lord decide! We thought we would offer $62,500 for the house and the furnishings. If the owner accepted our offer, we would go ahead, if not we would drop the plan. Well he did and we did! Thus began another wonderful adventure that lasted from 1991 to 2012.

For us, the Florida part of our adventure didn't really begin for five more years and in a way, those last years for me and for Singing Hills were the most important. The Chapel–Family Center was being completed amidst holdups and set-backs. The building had to be brought up to code, as did the leaching field. We had to contend with broken pipes and a myriad of other winter problems and, oh, yes, the wood fires had to be kept burning. The winters really produced some interesting scenarios. On one occasion, as I was getting ready to go to bed, the fire alarm system in the Family Center went off. We had a computerized signal board which showed the location of the alarm and which also notified the fire department. We also had a keyboard located in the small store area. As I rushed through the lodge, I found all the Mennonite folks in the lodge dining room, everyone dressed in night clothes. They had followed the instructions to a "T."

If the alarm sounds in your building, everyone is to go to the meeting room in the next building.

But for me, the plan didn't go so well. There was no key on the keyboard in the store where it should have been. The door was locked where the alarm was sounding. There was nothing to do but to call our maintenance man at his home on the property and get ready for the volunteer fire department to arrive. He had a key on his key ring and we determined where the alarm was sounding.

At that very moment the fire chief appeared, with several others, all dressed in full gear. It didn't take long for them to determine that the problem was not a fire, but a faulty alarm. After sending the guests, including many families back to their accommodations, I had the whole night to reflect on the "what if" of the experience. At least the next time we would not have the same problem.

Sometimes it seemed like the Lord didn't want me go to bed. One frigid night I was about to close the drapes on our large picture window when I saw a lot of red and blue flashing lights at the bottom of the tubing hill. I knew immediately that something really serious had happened and that it would help to have the floodlights turned on to light the scene. The switch was mounted on the big maple tree near the bottom of the tubing hill. Pulling on a jacket, I headed down the hill but had to contend with knee-deep snow with a half-inch frozen crust.

When the lights came on there appeared to be a drastic situation. There was a small group of girls who had been screaming and were being loaded into an ambulance. It seems that they had broken the rules about snow-tubing after hours and especially in the dark, without supervision. Our rules for the hill were simple: When the lights went out, the hill was closed and definitely there were to be no chain groups at any time. But they had formed a chain to come down from the top. The hill, being crusted with ice, was extremely fast and they had fallen off the tubes and slid along the icy surface, out of control. Some had scratched their faces on the ice and there was blood visible. After a more careful examination by the emergency personnel, it was determined that all of the injuries were superficial, but the girls were of course worried about their facial injuries. The leaders did acknowledge their mistake but it would be something I would long remember!

During those years we had snowmobiles for awhile and we had at least ten of them for rental purposes. We had to be extremely careful with them and had another rule that guests using them would have to stay in a controlled line with one of our staff leading the way and another at the rear. We had a trail groomer and used it to prepare the snowmobile trails. On one particular winter weekend, we had a large Chinese group there for a retreat. They came from the Chinese Evangelical church of Boston. Most of them were college students and had recently come from China. Only a few actually spoke or understood English. Before allowing guests to use the snowmobiles, either I or another staff member had a pre-ride instruction meeting where it was explained how to operate the machines and especially the trail ride rules.

Well, the group started out and the instructor and I returned to the workshop, which was located in the garage of our house. It had a good view of the hill and driveway and suddenly we saw a very strange sight.

Two snowmobiles were heading down the driveway with no riders! They were kept in the road by the snow banks on each side, but where would they end up with no riders? At the bottom of the drive, there was a turn toward Stage Road and when the machines arrived there, they both went off into the brush and stalled. No damage done! Evidently we learned that the girls who had been riding them had panicked and just jumped off. Shortly after that, the insurance company notified us that we could no longer let our guests use the machines because of liability. However, our staff used them to good purpose for getting from one job to another.

Memories, Memorials, and Many Special Friends

Mom and Dad

M Y MOM AND DAD were quite content with their Hillside apartment and needed only minimal help and care in the beginning. However, it was evident that Mom was slipping physically, and mentally, as well. The many years of struggling with her serious thyroid condition had

My parents enjoyed living at Singing Hills.

taken their toll. But one of the neat things for me was to look in on them in the evenings and see them sitting together on the couch, watching the TV and holding hands. This is what marriage is all about. It soon became evident that Mom would be bedridden most of the time. My mother, Mary Pultze Jones was born in Catskill, NY on March 8,

1897 and died at our home in the presence of the family and her doctor, Dr. Kowles, on August 12, 1988 at 91 years of age.

At my mother's funeral held in Bridgeport, CT, Dave did a wonderful service with his thoughts and comments to say goodbye at the service. She was a wonderful mother to me and a special grandmother to our children. Although her death was not a shock to Dad or to us, it was a sad time in our family, but the living arrangements, with Dad keeping most of his own independence, made it easier. Dad ate meals with us and kept occupied with his daily *New York Times*, TV, and his car for daily outings. Our main task was to help him to feel useful and motivated.

In the meantime, what was going on in the Florida house? Marian and I were able to take our vacations in late spring during the mud season in New Hampshire, when there were fewer guests at Singing Hills, and sometimes in the late fall when business was slower. Don was beginning to take on more responsibility and it was becoming obvious that he had the spiritual and mental "stuff," and the vision needed to not just carry on, but to take Singing Hills to greater heights. In the winter seasons, we rented the house to friends: Bill and Jayne Bush and friends of friends. Bill had been a member of the Singing Hills Board of Directors and owned a music business. He gave Singing Hills a generous reduction in the cost of a beautiful Kawai Baby Grand Piano for the main chapel where it still remains. The balance of the cost came as memorial contributions in memory of Marian's mother, Lois Miller, in 1980. Speaking of memorials, the children's playground located next to the entrance road is a memorial to Jonathan,

The Jonathan Biebel Memorial playground

our grandson. It was launched using funds that had been given to his parents during his illness and after his death.

I think I can honestly say that my enthusiasm and vision for the Singing Hills ministry did not diminish during those last years of 1988-1991. However, to make a move from Plainfield, NH, to a totally different lifestyle in Sebastian, FL, required a lot of thinking and planning. I tried to lay the whole thing out on the table, including our prospective financial budget and the actual physical part of the move. It had to be a plan that Singing Hills could handle, as well as one that would be a minimum necessary budget for us.

At the Board of Directors meeting on May 26, 1990, I tendered my resignation as President and Chairman of the Board. This was accompanied by a recommendation that Don Jordan should replace me in those posts and that Leif Arvidson be nominated and elected as Vice President. The resignation was accompanied by a plan whereby Marian and I could continue working at Singing Hills from late May or early June until October. Our capacity would be to help with fund raising. Marian would help with office work and I would work on the grounds, as well. We would be actually earning about $12,000.00 of our $20,000.00 retirement. The report that I prepared for the Board included financial information about our compensation.

The final figures showed that for the eighteen years of service with both Marian and I working full-time, we had received a total of $135,728.93 in cash and benefits, an average of $7,540.50 per year. In a quote from that report I wrote, "We want you to know that through hard work and the Lord's loving care we have had eighteen wonderful years and our lives have been abundantly cared for. I just hope that young people in the future will be able to have a vision and through faith and hard work, realize its fulfillment."

On the personal side, we were trying to envision what it would be like in Florida and what we would need financially. One gift that the Lord gave me was the ability to foresee budgeting factors, both in regard to the churches we served, Singing Hills, and our own personal finances. Without considering the special unforeseen blessings we received, our proposed personal budget always came out within 5 percent of being accurate at the end of each year. Our tithe was always at the head of the line in expense and next there were set income and expense items that we could count on. The bottom line is that we would need an income of about $35,000.00 per year to cover all the projected expense including the house mortgage. Our $20,000.00 retirement pension from Singing Hills, Social Security, Dad's contribution (he would live with us), and other sources would do it.

Paul Dubey was a member of our staff for several years and was instrumental in the installation of the leaching field for the Hillside House. He later married Sandy Otten, one of our Board members. Together with myself and Bill Jordan, we prepared and planted the surface of the field and we produced a field that has stood the test of time and weather. It was Paul Dubey who accompanied me on one of our first visits to Florida to get the house prepared. We flew on Southwest airlines and our arrival was in Orlando. This became a frequent choice for us through the years because of the direct flight from Manchester. I remember my very first fishing in Florida. Paul and I took the sixteen-foot-long used boat that I had purchased out to a small island in the Indian River. We beached the boat and fished off the sandbar that ex-

Believe it or not, that's bait I used once

tended out into the river. It was exciting and I immediately fell in love with Florida fishing.

Our trips to Florida became more frequent and we took my Dad with us for our first extended stay for the winter. It was his first airplane flight and provided a chance for him to view New York City from the air. New York had been Dad's favorite place earlier in his life. His office had been in the Chrysler building and those lunches in Battery Park while watching the ships in New York harbor had been a wonderful time for him. Everything was coming up roses for him until that terrible day in October 1929—the day the stock market crash ushered in the Great Depression. Somehow, Dad had become a friend of Eddie Rickenbacher, famous for his rescue at sea after his plane was shot down. He had invited Dad to his office in LaGuardia airport where he was president and CEO of Eastern Airlines. Dad took me with him and, there as a young man, I had the opportunity to shake the hand of this famous hero of World War II.

During our early time in Florida we had a lot to learn. There was investigation of where to shop; what bank to use; also about auto repair and service; medical service, and which church to attend? Our main interest though was the housing development that we lived in. It consisted of fifty lots and forty-nine homes, and as mentioned earlier, a recreation area adjacent to the Sebastian River with a boat launch and dock. It was a lovely place but did have its problems related mostly to the water supply and sewer due to the fact that the developer had abandoned any part in dealing with those problems.

Another negative was the fact that our community was in a direct path to the local airport runway. Small planes were landing and taking off right over our homes, sometimes so low that we could distinctly see the pilot's face. It didn't take us long to become acclimated to Sebastian and Florida weather. We found that all of our neighbors were friendly, in fact the whole town seemed that way to us. Our home was located just three miles from a shopping center, and the hospital was only a short drive down Roseland Road and we could be there in a matter of minutes. This proved to be a good thing because in the years ahead we would often need the hospital.

One of the first things we did with the house was to convert the garage into a private room for Dad. We found that in the rear portion of the garage, there were all the plumbing connections to create a medium-sized bathroom with shower. Thus that area became a private room with bath and shower.

When we first arrived at River's Edge, Fred Hoffman and his wife, Kathy, were instrumental in getting important issues settled for the community. At that time River's Edge was part of Sebastian, but separated from the rest of the city by the airport and other large wooded areas; as a result, our development had no city services. Through extra hard work and dealings with the state of Florida, Fred had been able to get the legislature in Tallahassee to grant us secession from the city of Sebastian and to become a self-governing entity. That affected just about everything, including taxes and especially decision making. The Homeowners Association had by-laws, met at certain designated dates for election of officers, and to vote on important decisions pertaining to the development. In one instance, this included dealing with the poor water quality which was provided from a shallow well, as well as the sewage plant located across Roseland Road, which had frequent breakdowns.

Fortunately, it wasn't long before Indian River County decided to put in water and sewer lines to extend along Roseland Road and we could be connected to both by paying an impact fee. For us, the fee would only be half of what others were paying because the county used our sewage plant temporarily while the piping was being installed along the road. So, we ended up with all underground piping and wiring, great features.

Inside and outside the house we were making as many improvements as we could with very limited resources. Converting the garage into a bedroom was a major expense. The front entrance at that time was through a small veranda with partial masonry walls, layered with stucco, as was the whole house. There was a garden area that was hard to keep so we decided to close the area floor with concrete, have a metal roof and screen-in the front, with a screen door. It made a pleasant sitting area and later on became a waiting room for Marian's piano students and parents.

We had a neighbor who approached me about putting in a small shared dock where we could moor our boats, one on each side and I agreed. There was a small island just off the recreation area where the developer had planned to put in fifty docks and he had a permit to do so from the Army Corps of Engineers. The permit was good for ten years. However, that date had expired so we applied for and received a renewal permit. For some time, we and our neighbors enjoyed the dock, which was installed by a dock building company. While this was happening, the environmental movement was gathering steam and one day we received notice that our docks would have to be removed. So, as a community, we were battling on two issues: the dock situation and our effort to have the runway situation at the airport resolved.

Our cause received attention as a result of a tragic collision that occurred directly overhead when two planes met in mid-air and plummeted straight down. One landed just across the street in Charlie Stevens' yard and the other came down behind the fence of the old sewage plant on Roseland Road. Charlie Stevens, who became a good friend, was sitting on his back porch when he heard the collision and saw the plane nose-dive into his yard. He rushed to see if he could help but found that the young pilot was clearly dead. Across Roseland Road the emergency crews extracted the other pilot. He was badly injured but survived. One young girl had witnessed the actual collision and it was determined that the former Air Force pilot was at fault, having cut in on the flight path of the young student.

Marian and I were not there at the time but there was an important sequel to it. One afternoon, as I was working around the yard, I noticed a group of people clustered around the hole in Charlie's yard where the plane had nose-dived. Almost immediately I recognized that this must be the family of the young man who had died there. I approached them and said how sorry all of us were for their loss. I explained that I was a Pastor and Chaplain and had a short prayer with them. I later wrote a letter offering comfort from God's Word and also a copy of Dave's book *Jonathan, You Left Too Soon*. I received a treasured letter in return. The following is the letter dated January 21, 1990 and with it was a photo of the young man who had died in the crash.

Jeff Dimond died needlessly in an airplane crash

Dear Rev. Biebel,

I am touched by the Christian love you extended to my family and by your sharing of your personal loss. One way we have learned to cope with Jeff's death is certainly the knowledge that others have experienced a pain so deep. It has been especially helpful to me to know you were nearby during the many hours that Jeff was left in his plane. I sincerely hope your prayers were given, not only for Jeff, but for your friends and neighbors whose safety was a concern.

Jeff was our first son, and middle child. He would have been twenty-one this March 16. He was a sincere, caring person with many friends, a faith in God, a zest for life, and always a positive approach to life and his future. He had been a private pilot during the later years of high school and lived and breathed his future in the air. It is beyond belief that our son was killed by a man so careless, so disrespectful of the very rules and policies of safety in the air—the very rules Jeff had learned himself and followed so carefully. He had taken his sister flying a few months before his death and had assured her that she was safer in the air than on the ground. I miss him so.

My family and I appreciate the copy of your son's book as well as Dr. Dobson's magazine. We are very familiar with Dr. Dobson's ministry, and although we do receive his "Focus on the Family" magazine, we had never seen the "Physician." It is of particular interest as my husband practices Internal Medicine.

I have been reading Dave's book this week as well as preparing for a Disciple study class on Job. I particularly focused on his statement that perhaps the true test of faith is our acceptance that we shall never receive some answers. I find depth and compassion in the book, as well as comfort. However, we still cry every day, attend memorials and dedications for Jeff and ask the same questions, anyway. Why Jeff?

I feel the need to send you a picture of our children—the last one of them together—Thanksgiving, 1989. Jeff stands between Emily and his younger brother, Jacob. Emily is finishing her Occupational Therapy studies at the Medical College of Georgia and graduated two years ago from Furman University. Jacob is a freshman at Furman, now. Both have had a difficult school year, to say the least, for our kids were great friends and supports for each other. I have also sent a few special printings to share with you. I hope you may feel some of the charisma that Jeff radiated.

I pray every day for God's presence to lead me. I pray that He will bless Jeff and keep him near to us. I am grateful to our many friends, as well as Jeff's who continue to nurture us. And, I do find gratification in the scholarship, tree dedications, church memorial, etc.

It is only because there are other Christians on this earth who have shared their love that I am able to move in a new direction. Our meetings at Compassionate Friends and our counseling sessions are helpful, but God is my only true strength.

Thank you for your letter and gifts. May God bless you for reaching out to a small family with the deepest of needs. And may He offer abundant love to you in your loss.

Sincerely,
Julie Dimond

Charlie and Annabelle Stevens were great neighbors. Charlie became my first fishing buddy, and Annabelle and Marian enjoyed many afternoons around their pool and they also enjoyed visiting Saturday morning yard sales and taking long walks together. Well, I had purchased a sixteen-foot-long boat called "the fishing skiff" and we would take all our tackle, a cooler with our lunch and cold drinks and head out for fishing. Sometimes we would go straight to the Sebastian Inlet and other times we would take the North fork of the Sebastian River. The Sebastian River state park was located on Route 1A and included camping and RV facilities. It had several paved launching ramps. It also had a long fishing dock that was always crowded with fishermen and women. The currents coming and going from the ocean were extremely strong and dangerous. It was not uncommon for boats to be swamped there, with the occupants needing to be rescued. Large yachts and commercial fishing boats frequently used this inlet to go out to the ocean or come in to dock. All this made that spot a place to learn and be careful.

The Indian River itself is part of the Inland Waterway that extends from Florida to Maine. It contains the most fish species in the world. As far as Charlie and I were concerned, we were especially good at losing hats, sinkers, and other things overboard. More often than not, we came in empty-handed but on one occasion while trolling the Sebastian River at the west end we each got a huge strike and one by one we pulled in a snook and a redfish, both the same exact size. That evening, the Stevens' invited us over for a fish dinner. Delicious!

One of the historical facts about the Indian River was that during World War II the river channel was dredged to allow tankers and freighters to go north or south without going up or down the coast along the ocean side of the Florida Shore. The German U Boats were having a picnic sinking ships before this project was completed. They would wait about ten miles out until one of our ships, usually a tanker, would come by nicely silhouetted by the glow from lights in Florida. Although there was a mandatory blackout, some light always showed and it was easy for a submarine to torpedo the ship with all its cargo and the many men who lost their lives.

Sometimes you get lucky and catch a redfish

When the Indian River was dredged to produce a twelve to fourteen foot deep channel, the material was put to the side and resulted in a whole series of "spoil islands." Over time, these became covered with vegetation and a refuge for all kinds of birds, especially pelicans. Each island had a sandbar caused by the changing tides and provided habitation for crabs, small fish, and every other sea creature. This is truly an exciting place!

As I mentioned earlier, Bill and Jayne Bush had rented our home for the winters before we moved permanently to Florida. They enjoyed the environment and lifestyle so much that they went on to rent a condo in a gated community called Pelican Point, from Clint and Charlotte

Brown, the friends who had initially introduced us to Florida. Bill and Jayne eventually purchased their own condo. The Browns also had a home in Garden Grove, on the outskirts of Vero Beach, where they spent their winters. Bill had a pilot's license and took me up from Sebastian airport for a look at our home and the area from the air. Bill and I did many things together. I took him fishing and he invited me to play tennis at Pelican Point. We played really hard and that went on several times a week until my knee said "no more." It was on one of our fishing trips that Bill and I ran into a school of big "blues" in the inlet, but we weren't alone. The boats, the current, and the Pelicans diving around us all produced a maelstrom but in the midst of it all Bill had a huge strike. It was crazy trying to maneuver among the boats with over 100 yards of line out and a ten pound, fighting, blue fish on the other end. We did finally land the fish but he wasn't ready to give up and flapped around in the bottom of the boat. We had to be extremely careful in subduing him because "blues" are known for their razor sharp teeth and are nicknamed "chompers."

I should mention that while we were battling the fish, the current pushed us into the breakwater, thankfully with no damage.

Back at River's Edge, we were getting ourselves and Dad settled into our nice, if modest, home at 7 Gail Road. The Hoffmans were spearheading the effort to have the airport move its main runway by restoring the East-West landing strip that had been used by the Army during World War II. Our group was not the only one asking for this change and the city officials of Sebastian acceded to the plan, which necessitated moving some hangers and other small buildings. In the end, though, it was a good move, not only for us but for the city. After the change, it wasn't long before "Sebastian Sky Dive" located at the airport and it became a daily occurrence to see parachutes descending. In some cases they miscalculated the landing zone and in at least two instances parachutists were killed. One of those was a man who landed in the Sebastian River and drowned and the other crashed through the roof of a local house. One day Marian was driving down Roseland Road to go shopping when she saw a sky diver coming down just ahead of her. She stopped and watched as the man's chute got tangled in overhead wires and he dropped to the ground. She called 911 on her cell phone but an emergency vehicle arrived on the scene almost immediately. One day our foursome had just teed off at the seventeenth hole at Sebastian golf course when a sky diver landed right on the tee we had just left.

On another subject: Among God's creatures, one of the worst has to be fire ants. Anyone who has had the miserable experience of stepping on a fire ant hill will never forget it. One day in Wabasso, FL, we stopped to look at some items in a yard sale and Marian stepped out of the car right onto a hill. Ouch!! It took emergency maneuvering to get them all off!

The Hoffmans, who had done so much for River's Edge, had decided to buy a new home in another location and were selling their house in River's Edge so Fred did not run for President again. So in May 1993 I was elected President of the Homeowners Association and served until October 1995. After a long drawn-out battle of correspondence and phone calls we lost the docks and I had to have them removed with help. It was no easy task. A strong rope had to be attached to the dock posts and to a pickup truck to give them the pull necessary to dislodge them from the mud and sand, but we did get it done. There was a horseshoe pit, not far from the remaining dock and some of the men had regular games every Thursday evening. On one of those occasions, I passed them on the way to the dock, to try my luck at fishing. On my very first cast, I caught a good sized snook, a favorite eating fish. The men who were playing horseshoes couldn't believe that!

Being President involved presiding over the two business meetings each year and bringing up subjects like insurance, property improvements, and assessment of the annual membership fee (which was extremely reasonable). The membership fees included lawn care of the common area, liability insurance, and whatever maintenance was necessary, as well as appointing a social committee to plan the two or three parties or picnics that were held each year for the homeowners. For all the years we spent at River's Edge, we had good neighbors almost 100 percent of the time. The one exception was when a house or two was rented out to indiscriminate people who had wild parties and no personal concern for the property or the peace of their neighbors.

As we were enjoying the first years of our retirement, our family was occupied in pursuits of their own. Paul and Kathy were busy with Biebel Builders Incorporated construction company in Windsor, VT, as well as with their children. Dan and Cheri had moved to Okeechobee, FL, where they both had acquired new teaching jobs with the thought in mind to be nearer to us. Marian and I made a number of preliminary trips to Okeechobee to find a nice home for them. They had no way to come there in advance of moving so they came along, sight unseen. We were able to help them and soon they were settled in to a southern lifestyle. A year or so later, they relocated to a much nicer home in the same development. A small lake in the backyard provided some nice bass fishing for Dan and he went on to bigger things on Lake Okeechobee itself with a boat he purchased. I accompanied him on several occasions. Those were exciting times.

Don and Judy devoted their time and efforts to the continuing development of Singing Hills. They were able to visit us a number of times and when they did it was

Don and Judy Jordan family

always picnics, beaches, fishing, and golf. They brought the girls with them, too, and we took them boating and for their first experience at fishing. One trip resulted in my showing them how "not" to remove a hook from a catfish. In doing it, I got stabbed by one of the prongs situated near the head and dropped a pair of pliers overboard. We had fun with the schools of dolphin that always played in the Indian River and on one occasion they surrounded the boat where we could photograph them.

All this time, Dad seemed happy spending much of his time in his easy chair and reading the *New York Times*, which we had subscribed to and had delivered to our newspaper box. He enjoyed going out to eat with us and an occasional walk around the nearby neighborhood. Dad was born on June 1905 and married my Mom on July 27, 1927. So, he was closing in on his eighty-eighth birthday in 1993.

My Dad enjoyed his 88th birthday celebration

Charles

One of the things that Dad did with me was to go on trips to visit Cousin Charles Carr who lived in Palm Coast, FL, 135 miles north of Sebastian. We would go for a visit and take Charles out to dinner. When we first arrived at his home and returned after eating at the nearby Denny's, we both couldn't help noticing that Charles wasn't maintaining his home and property. But he enjoyed the meal at Denny's. He would go to the salad bar and take a big helping from there, even before the waitress came. Then before we left for home, he always asked if we could get him some Granny Smith apples, and at Christmas he always wanted fruit cake (that was easy). We did wonder why he never invited us into the house to visit. I would find that out later!

Those trips with Dad were very important to me, providing a chance to talk about everything. But Dad's health was beginning to fail and in the last part of 1992 and beginning of 1993 it became obvious to us that he was suffering from heart failure. On numerous occasions I took him to the emergency room at Indian River Memorial Hospital in Vero Beach. On one occasion, it was late evening and Dad was having trouble breathing. I knew it was his heart and got him into the emergency room as quickly as possible. The area was crowded with people who had been in some kind of brawl and they were being attended to right away. I was upset because I knew Dad needed immediate care but even when our turn came, we had to do all that routine paperwork for insurance that we had previously done. Finally, they took him into a small room where he had to lay on a flat gurney. He was treated by an emergency room physician who was going to release him. I said, "Absolutely not," and finally persuaded them to admit Dad. He was in the hospital for a week and then discharged to come home. He required home health care almost round the clock. He needed a hospital bed, a night caregiver, and bathroom assistance. Marian and I both participated in this but, for the most part, I did the bathroom trips with him. His last trip to the hospital came on or about February 10, 1994.

His cardiac doctor was Dr. Janet Anderson and one afternoon they rushed Dad into a room for cardiac catheterization, while I waited in the hall. After a while Dr. Anderson came out to tell me that they had lost him during the procedure, but while we were talking one of the nurses came out and said that he had been revived. He was given oxygen and returned to his room where he finally did leave us on Valentine's Day, February 14, 1994. He was eighty-nine years old. Those years he had with us in Florida allowed me to be closer to him than all the years before.

During our twenty-one years in Florida, one thing that was always preeminent in our lives was our worship and service experiences. When we first visited the Vero Beach area, we attended the First Church of God, affiliated with the Indiana Group of musicians such as the Gaithers and Sandi Patti. It was a big church with lots of good music and a pastor, Tom Bates, who did preach the gospel. We became friends with Tom and his wife, Carol, but were sad later, when Tom resigned to enlist in a restoration program, an all too familiar scenario among evangelical pastors.

When we became permanent residents at our home in River's Edge, we began to attend Community Baptist Church which was just a short walk from our house. It was a relatively new Independent Baptist church and it was an enthusiastic, growing fellowship with a nice group of young and middle-aged people. We became friends with many of them. During the time we worshiped there I was asked to teach the adult Sunday school class and served on the finance committee. There was a need for a pianist, so Marian was right at home with that, and working with the choir. We appreciated the pastor's messages but as time went on we felt he made the mistake, often, of referring to the church as "his church." This led to one friend, a very astute business man, resigning from the finance committee because he also felt the pastor was too possessive.

Well, Dan and his family were visiting us (this was when the kids were still at home and they all still lived in Wyoming) and we were planning on a day trip to the Space Center, a drive of about seventy-five miles up I-95 to Merritt Island, FL. This same friend was kind enough to let us use his van for the trip and all seven of us fit very nicely in it. Arriving at the Space Center, we visited the IMAX Theater where we felt like we were actually taking off with the Apollo rocket. Then, we took the tour bus around the whole area, including the launch site and viewed the array of rockets on display. Then, after food at the cafeteria, it was time to head home and we all piled back into the van and headed back to I-95. We were well on our way, having passed the Titusville exit, and were on a stretch of road with nothing but speeding cars and trucks when the motor quit! Have you ever felt that sinking feeling? This was it! It was getting dark; we had a van full of family and a dead car!

Wait! There was a police barracks and shooting range directly across the Interstate but it was surrounded by a heavy wire fence. To get to the other side of I-95 would take great care, time, and patience. It seemed like there would never be a break in the traffic, but I finally made it. Going up to the fence, I tried to attract the attention of the officers who were intently focused on using the shooting range. Finally one of them saw me and approached, whereupon I told him of our dire circumstance. He promised to call the Sheriff whom he said would be there in no time. I re-crossed I-95 and told the family the good news. However, the Sheriff never came and we were left to fend for ourselves. The twilight was turning into dark and huge trucks were passing with a swishing sound. I finally decided that our best bet was for me to go back on the road several hundred yards and hitchhike. I borrowed a white sweater from Marian, one that would show up far enough ahead to enable someone to stop. So there I was beside the highway flapping the sweater and believe it or not, it was only a short time when a man in a small pickup pulled up and offered to take us to Viera, FL.

So, Marian and Cheri squeezed into the front seat and the rest of us climbed into the small six-foot pickup bed and soon we were at the Viera exit where we all disembarked and thanked the gracious man. There was a Burger King restaurant there and everyone was famished so the first order of business was to get some food. Next, I called my friend and explained the situation. The van was parked about seven miles from an exit or entrance in either direction. There were seven of us! He said that he and his wife would each bring a car and meet us at the restaurant. In the meantime, I should call a tow truck, which I did. I found a possible tow at a Vero Beach location but was told the truck was already out on another call. He would come as soon as possible.

When my friend and his wife arrived she loaded all six of the family somehow into her car and headed for home. He and I waited for the tow truck, which arrived in short order. But in order for the driver to get to the van, he had to go north on I-95, get off at the exit, then enter the south lane and drive the seven miles south to it. Cecil and I were already there, awaiting him. I got in the van, turned the key and "Oh, no," the lights went on—but only for several seconds. So the van was pulled onto the flat bed with a cable and I accompanied the driver to

Vero Beach Ford, where it would stay. It needed a new alternator. My friend drove me home and that ended our Space Center adventure.

We subscribed to the *Vero Beach Press Journal* daily newspaper and one day Marian noticed an ad for a piano player at Forest Park Baptist Church. She answered the ad, auditioned, and was hired. This was an easy way for us to move from Community Baptist. Thus began a whole new long-term chapter in our spiritual lives and opportunity for service. Forest Park was a fairly large church with adequate facilities. Paul Mace was the pastor and we were pleased with his Scripture-oriented messages. During the next seventeen years we would do just about everything—preach, teach, be a deacon, develop an adult fellowship, and help with the music ministry. It would be our pleasure to meet and befriend many good people. The highlights of that period were the mission trips north to do volunteer work at Singing Hills. On one occasion, the group consisted of Rick and Marlene Donnon and Esther and Paul Nightingale. On another it was Don and Melba Wolverton and David and Carrie Mace, the pastor's son and daughter-in-law. What a great job they did with cleaning, painting, and cutting trees and brush. Don and David completed deck and roof projects. Simmons and Irene Arthur and Barbara and Ed Depew came at another time. It was Simmons who helped raise the funds for the trip by providing fish for the fish fries, doing the cooking, and also organizing spaghetti dinners and a rummage sale.

Don and Melba Wolverton helped in many ways during their mission trip to Singing Hills

Sometime during that period, our son Dave, who lived in Colorado, called to tell me that he had met Jim Watson Jr., the son of Jim Sr., who had been the pastor before me in the Meriden Baptist Church. It was Jim Sr. who had taught me how to fish the streams for trout. I learned that the best place in a small river or stream was not still water but right in those eddies in the rapids. Jim, Jr. lived in Victor, CO, and had purchased land in an area where the Colorado gold rush had occurred many years before. He was convinced that he could open a gold-producing mine and had begun the process with a tower and open shaft, as well as a processing plant. He needed capital to continue and Dave, ourselves, and Simmons all invested sizable amounts in the projects. We knew that Jim was a Christian and a man determined to get the job done. He was also pastor of a small Baptist Church, as well as being Mayor of the town of Victor.

Simmons and Irene accompanied Marian and me on a memorable trip to Victor, which was at one time the highest livable town in the USA. Jim took us down the shaft to a level where he had opened a tunnel and he already had a rail track for a small car, designed to haul material. It was quite an experience for me, being that far underground. We went a distance into the tunnel to a place where he showed us pieces of stone that had been removed by a drill. Jim was looking for a vein of gold. Years before, the mother lode had been discovered and millions of dollars' worth of gold had been removed from mines in that area. Denver and especially Colorado Springs had been developed with that money before World War II.

Earlier (1990), Dan and Cheri had taken us on a wonderful trip into the Rockies. Dan had rented a van for the trip that would take us through Yellowstone National Park. They were still living in Sheridan, Wyoming. We took Lindsay with us, too, since we thought she would enjoy visiting with Heather. We saw elk, moose, and lots of wildlife. Old

Faithful was right on schedule for us and the walk among the bubbling hot springs was a treat. One thing we'll never forget, though, is our trip back to Dan's on the Bear Tooth Mountain highway, a twisting, turning road that went all the way to the mountain top at 11,000 feet. There was a rest stop at the summit and then it was down the treacherous road toward Red Lodge, Montana, and our next stop. Starting down the sharp grade, the red engine light suddenly came on. Emergency, or not, we finally made it down and entered the town of Red Lodge, which was just like the towns in the wild west movies of that period. The problem with the car turned out to be the catalytic converter, which had been affected by the high altitude.

After having some much needed food, we headed for Billings, MT, and then back toward Sheridan, WY. On the way, we stopped at the Custer Battlefield National Monument. We arrived in time for a historic talk by a park attendant who explained how and where the battle occurred. In that battle, General George Custer, with a contingent of 210 Union soldiers came to the place called "Little Big Horn." It was here that all of Custer's soldiers, except one, were killed by a far superior number of Indians. All of the soldiers except Custer, himself, were scalped and left lying on the field. Today, there are white crosses marking the burial sites of the lost men. After perusing the battlefield and the souvenir shop, we were on the last lap back to Sheridan. What a wonderful trip it had been!

One of our most exciting trips was to Powhatan Plantation in Williamsburg, VA, to celebrate our 50th Wedding Anniversary with our family. Our flight from Orlando took us to Norfolk where we rented a car and drove the fifty or so miles to the "time share" accommodations that Don and Judy had provided for the whole family to enjoy for the week. What a great time we had with a cookout in the reserved pavilion, and lots of family pictures were taken. We played golf at a course in Newport News where deer were constantly crossing the fairway. The unusual feature of that was a pure white albino deer amongst the others,

Most of our family celebrated our 50th Anniversary with us

a very rare sight. The family was free to divide up for sightseeing during the day and we got back together in the evenings. We went to the Maritime Museum in Newport News where we saw a whole array of ship models. Some visited the historic sites in the area, others went to Busch Gardens for excitement and some went into Washington, D.C., for a day. We were sorry to miss Dave whose marriage to Ann had ended and he was moving on to marry again. Marian and I had adopted a policy, early on, not to attempt to interfere in the lives of our children, who were now adults on their own paths. It was similar to my earlier decision to make a "clean break" with the churches I had pastored, after I left. We would be "encouragers" but not "interferers."

After a wonderful time, Marian and I headed to Norfolk for our flight back to Orlando. It was Sunday morning and we were there in the terminal waiting in plenty of time. However, the desk attendant came on the speaker to announce that the plane was overbooked and that volunteers who could wait for the next flight in about two hours would be given vouchers for free trips and an upgrade to first class. So, we accepted the offer and were on our way home on the next flight.

Again, it was very late! Getting home is always a warm and wonderful feeling except in this case, it was to discover that the house was locked and we did not have the key. My only hope was that a window had been left unlocked and sure enough, the last one I tried opened after I removed the screen. So I climbed in, went through the house and opened the carport door for Marian. As she entered we turned on the kitchen light only to find a huge black spider in the middle of the floor and we noticed an accumulation of water on the floor in the laundry room. What a reception! Get the spider, worry about the water in the morning, and fall into bed, exhausted but still happy!

As I mentioned earlier, we had become good friends with Simmons and Irene Arthur. They had moved from Vero Beach, where we met them, to retire and purchase a very nice home in Frostproof, FL. It was at the top of one of the few hills in Florida and had a beautiful view of the surrounding area. One of the frequent Florida hurricanes, "Hurricane David," was approaching our area in Sebastian, so Simmons and Irene invited us to come and bring two widowed ladies with us from our neighborhood. Fran and Betty were living alone and apprehensive. Thus, we evacuated before the storm and took all our perishable food with us. We had beautiful, private accommodations at the Arthur household and plenty to eat.

On the day that the hurricane was projected to hit, Simmons and I decided to play a round of golf and upon arrival at the course, we had it all to ourselves. As we teed off on the first hole the sun was shining and for the first five holes, the weather was great. However, after teeing off on the sixth hole, a sudden change occurred with blasts of wind and sheets of rain. That was it for golfing during a hurricane! The storm, though, wasn't as strong as predicted and later the next afternoon, we headed back to River's Edge and found that there was no damage done. Thank you, Lord!

Sometime after, Simmons found that he had an aggressive case of prostate cancer and even though he sought treatment at one of the best hospitals in the U.S., in Tampa, FL, he lost the battle after a valiant fight during which he continued as long as possible to serve the Lord. When Simmons died, I wrote what I thought about him as a fellow Christian and friend:

There was a special man who loved the Lord with all his heart. He was a man, just enough rough around the edges to make you admire his convictions. At the same time, he was a man with a kind and loving heart, one bursting with cheerfulness and giving. He had a very special calling—a gift given to him by God Himself. He was called to share the gospel and God's love through missions and personal witnessing. When ill health overtook him, he stood strong in his faith and continued to the end, serving, trusting, and witnessing as long as life permitted. He fought a wonderful fight and he kept the faith. The kingdom of God and the fellowship of believers and especially his friends will surely miss him, but he will surely be welcomed by Jesus with the words reserved for special people, "Well done, good and faithful servant." Oh, yes, his name was Simmons Arthur and he was a special friend of mine, and he will not be forgotten.

From Warren Biebel – April 24, 2003

Memories, Memorials, and Many Special Friends

After Simmons' death, Irene moved to a small apartment in Lake Wales and for a long time, we kept in touch with her by phone.

We had made other friendships, both in River's Edge and in Forest Park Baptist Church. One couple among those was Ed and Barbara Depew. They made a trip to Singing Hills to help celebrate an anniversary and Barb took extensive pictures, both at Singing Hills and on a side trip up Mt. Ascutney, in Vermont. We had a picnic after climbing the tower at the mountain's peak. We could look down on the whole area including the home of our son, Paul, in Brownsville, VT.

I joined Ed and Saylor Runyon for a weekly game of golf at Dodger Pines, a small course in Vero Beach. Ed went on to be a regular at the Men's Golf League at Sandridge Golf Course in Vero Beach. Marian was able to take up golf for a few years with Susie Runyon, Irene, and Barb Depew at a Par 3, nine hole course in Wabasso, FL, where they played on Tuesday mornings and had a very enjoyable time together. That group broke up because Irene and Simmons retired and moved away, Susie's husband took ill and died suddenly while they were on a trip, and as time went by, Barb, who had a wonderful, outgoing, bubbly personality, became a victim of Alzheimer's disease and Ed found it necessary to have a caregiver stay with her during his own weekly game of golf. Barb passed away in 2014.

Al Husosky had invited me to join a foursome at the Men's Golf League at Sandridge golf course. Sandridge consisted of two eighteen-hole county courses; the "Lakes" and the "Dunes." What a privilege it was for me to be able to play every Tuesday at such great courses, with good friends. Both of the courses were kept in top-notch condition but provided quite a challenge to mediocre golfers like me. However, during the thirteen years that I played there, I did win the club championship once. A special event happened for me on June 12, 2012 on the fourteenth hole of the 'Dunes" course. I took out my three wood and sank the shot, 147 yards from the tee for my second (and last) hole in one. There was a tidy monetary prize of $330.00. And I also received a nice note from my partner Dick Cahoy:

Warren,

Congrats are in order for accomplishing such a marvelous feat, and I was so fortunate to have been a witness. It was exciting.

Your Friend,

Dick

My golf mementos—two aces and D Flight Club Champion

At the time I made that shot I was eighty years old. The thing about golf that was most important was not my scores but the many friends and the great interplay and fun while keeping a spirit of competition. The original foursome consisted of Dick Wagner, Joe Truman, Al Hususky, and me—three great guys to have as friends. Yes, we took our golf seriously, but fun and good-natured quips served to make every game, no matter how good or bad, a pleasure. For example, on the "Lakes" ninth hole, Joe seemed to hit or land in the proximity of a certain pineapple palm tree quite often and on one occasion his ball landed in one of the outcropping leaf stems, too high to retrieve (not unusual). From that time on, that was "Joe's Tree."

On another occasion we had finished our round and were having our usual lunch in the clubhouse when Dick got an urgent call from his wife. She had been working around the front yard and somehow had lost her diamond wedding ring. Could Dick come home and help her search for it? I offered to help, too, so shortly we both were down on our hands and knees, feeling in the grass and bushes, without any luck. I had a brainstorm shortly thereafter and asked if she had checked the vacuum cleaner, having cleaned the house earlier. Sure enough, mixed in with the dirt and lint was the $3,000.00 diamond ring.

Golfing gave me some great friends

Sometimes our foursome, especially in late spring or summer, would travel to other courses to play. One of those was "Fairwinds," a challenging course south of Vero Beach. For our group, any score in the low 90s was pretty special but on one particular day, something happened to me that I can't explain. It seemed that almost every shot I took did just what I wanted it to. July 14, 1998 was a highlight for me in my golfing career. I wound up with a score of 83 but the real thrill came on the 167-yard fourteenth hole where my ball was straight and true and ended up in the hole for a treasured hole-in-one, my first one. Another time we traveled to West Palm Beach to play the PGA of America course there, and once again it turned out to be a special day for me on a professional course. Playing from the white tees on the north course, I wound up with a score in the 80s.

The World Golf Village and Golf Hall of Fame were located near Saint Augustine, FL, and on one of our trips to see Charles, we visited it and were approached by a person who was intent on having us attend a meeting where we could learn the advantages of buying a "timeshare." If we attended with no obligations, we would receive a ticket to the IMAX theater, a free round of golf for two, a $50.00 coupon for a seafood restaurant, and a two-night three-day stay in the timeshare accommodation. We couldn't resist the benefits but we didn't buy in. So, later, we invited Paul and Stephanie to join us while we were there. Paul and I played two rounds of golf and Marian and Steph went shopping and played miniature golf that went with the facilities.

An interesting thing happened on the second hole each day. On day one, Paul and I were paired with another golfer who appeared to be very good. As we approached the second hole, there was a course representative near the tee who offered us a deal. We could invest $5.00, $10.00, $20.00, or more and if we hit the green on the short Par 3 we would double our money. I wasn't going to do it but Paul said; "Oh, let's try," so all three of us invested ten dollars each. Paul and the other fellow shot and missed the green, and when my turn came, I hit the green and received a certificate for $20.00. On the second day, the scenario was repeated only this time we invested a larger amount and once again I miraculously hit the green. I ended up with coupons worth $90.00. The only catch was that they were only good for the pro shop and the prices there were high so I ended up with a "T" shirt, a hat, and a dozen balls. Oh, well! We had a good time and that really is what golf is all about. In the evening, we toured historic St. Augustine with the girls and enjoyed the museums and night lights.

Me, with sons Paul, Dave, and Dan

In addition to my regular foursomes, golf was a family affair, both in Florida and home in New England. Some of the best times in my life were the times I played with my three sons and my son-in-law. It was with one, sometimes two and on rare occasions, four of us together. We were always highly competitive but all in good humor and whenever possible, if we won: rubbing it in! The last time I played with my three sons, was February 19, 2011, on the "Lakes" course at Sandridge Golf Course. It was a pretty competitive day, with the individual competition not being settled until the last shot was made. You'd have to ask them who won by making a "sand save" and one-putt at the end. Maybe you should just ask Dave. Dan and Paul might not remember it as well as their older brother does.

Joe Truman, one of the original foursome, had skin trouble and had a number of surgeries. It was after a number of years that he was found to have aggressive melanoma (skin cancer) which, in the end, took his life. I felt honored to be asked by Mrs. Truman to participate in his memorial service. Al Husosky accompanied me. Two of our golfing buddies had left us! The Lord had a way of bringing people into my life and Dick Cahoy, a new member of the men's club, joined our foursome, along with a variety of other players.

The last foursome I played with regularly

By then, I was in my early 80s and Al didn't hesitate to "rub it in." He was about five years younger than me. But I continued to play pretty good golf and won my share of the prize money, which was based on the lowest weekly score after handicap was figured in. Dick later joined an earlier tee-off time group. Then something really special happened. Two new friends, Jim Greene and Al Worden came to make up a foursome with Al Husosky and me and this group would be with me until I finally had to call it a day (not for physical reasons but because we were moving back to New Hampshire). Jim Greene was a World War II veteran and had participated in invasion landings in the Pacific. He was in excellent health and drove the ball long and mostly straight. He and his wife, Jan, had been married many years. Besides being a good golfer, Jim was a good guy on the golf course and off the course. He was funny and pleasant.

It wasn't until I had been playing with Al Worden for some time that I found that he was a former (and famous) astronaut, the Commander of the vehicle that circled the moon while Scott and Irwin walked on the surface. It was Al's job to return and pick them up. That was Apollo 15. Al wrote a book of poems named, *Hello Earth*. In it he

Earthrise taken by Astronaut Commander Al Worden

A signed copy of his official NASA photo

described his feelings before, during the ascent, while alone in the vehicle, and landing again to pick up his fellow astronauts and the return to earth. It was while he circled alone around the moon that Al was moved to write: "One thing is certain, God did it all!" Al and his wife, Jill, had a home in Michigan and they enjoyed summers there and winters in Vero Beach. Jill fell ill to cancer and in spite of the very best treatment; it finally took her life on May 4, 2014. After an interlude, Al was back to golf but that was after I had moved away, myself. It was an honor for me to have known Al and I did the best I could to show Christ's love to him. I treasure his friendship and the astronautical mementos that he gave me.

Another kind of recreation that both Marian and I enjoyed was bowling. For a number of years, friends from Forest Park Church joined us every Friday night at the Vero Bowl for an evening of bowling and Fellowship. Bill Mawhinney, Rick and Marlene Donnon, Paul and Esther Nightingale, and many others joined us from time to time. Rick and Marlene were excellent bowlers and had many trophies to prove it. Marian enjoyed the bowling and we bought her a new ball and shoes. She and I arrived early one Friday and while we were changing shoes, a man I recognized walked by. He was very familiar to me, as a Red Sox fan, so I approached him and asked, "Are you who I think you are?" He said, "Yes," and I proceeded to get the autograph of Derek Lowe. He also invited me to attend the preseason game the next day in which he would be the starting pitcher. I knew the game was sold out—Red Sox vs. Dodgers—so I didn't give it another thought until I received a phone call from Paul Mace, my pastor. His house roof had been damaged by the recent hurricane and a group of volunteers were working to repair it. One was a lady who had five box seat tickets to that game and she had offered them to Pastor Mace. He in turn knew that I was a big fan and offered them to me so I drove to Vero and got them.

I tried to think of four other people to take them but came up empty, so it was on to the park for me with the five tickets. When I arrived, large crowds were entering and there were some people along the entrance area trying to sell tickets. I joined them, only I intended to give the tickets away. Pretty soon a couple came by and asked about the tickets. I said, "I'd like to give you these two tickets." They said, "No way," and insisted that they pay me face value, which was $15.00 each. The same scenario occurred a few minutes later when another couple came by. The bottom line was, that I, and the two other couples, had box seats for the game and I was ahead by $60.00. Derek Lowe started the game and also started a game in the 2004 World Series when he went seven innings with only eighty-five pitches. In that World Series, the Sox won their first championship in eighty-six years.

I became a Red Sox fan in 1949, and have remained one ever since. So, I had a special thrill on June 12, 2003, when our son Paul, arranged for tickets to a Red Sox–Cardinal game. He had become a good friend of a minority owner of the Red Sox who made it possible for me to have one of the best seats in Fenway. Paul had built a home for him on Killington Mountain in Vermont. My seat was in section 21, Row 1, seat one, right behind the backstop, a few feet from home plate. It was

What a thrill it was to see my name on the big screen at Fenway Park

interesting to see Tim Wakefield's knuckle ball dipping and dancing. To my great surprise, Paul had made arrangements so that, between the fourth and fifth innings, the Red Sox congratulated me for being a fan for forty-nine years, with my picture on the big screen in right center field. What a thrill and honor!

New Directions, Opportunities, and Blessings

BEGINNING IN 1994, MY LIFE TOOK A DIFFERENT DIRECTION FOR THE next eight years. Dad had passed away that year and Marian and I were doing all we could to improve our home and property at 7 Gail Road. In addition to being president of River's Edge, I had become maintenance man for five of our neighbors. They were only too glad to have me cut their grass and maintain their hedges every week. On my part, I appreciated the income which helped to pay for my Husqvarna tractor and other power tools. Marian was busy giving piano lessons at all hours of the day and sometimes in the evenings, at our home. At one time she had thirty students, when the public school made time for her in the after school program, once a week. She not only gave the lessons but catered an exceptional recital party for students and parents each spring. This was the means for her to buy a new white piano.

―᭜―

We still enjoyed having visitors: Among them were Harry and Joann Dopson and Bill and Alice Jordan. It was Bill who discovered a coral snake in our side yard, very colorful but extremely poisonous. Harry Dopson had given me two deep sea rods with conventional reels. These were designed for deep sea fishing but I was out trolling in the Sebastian River one day with Charlie. One of the rods was in place and trolling when the line suddenly caught on something on the bottom and the rod was yanked overboard. It took real ingenuity to put a three-way hook, part of a heavy sinker on the other rod and then drag it slowly in the area until we finally hooked the line and were able to retrieve the rod.

Some of our great neighbors from River's Edge

During those years in River's Edge, we had great neighbors. Among them were Lamar and Lois Bell, good Christian friends. He had been the fire chief in West Palm Beach before retirement. Len and Dottie Brown had built a new home on the corner where Len pursued his woodworking and model ship-building hobbies in their two-car garage. Len had retired from GE where he participated in working on propulsion systems of nuclear submarines. Most of the other folks got together at the fourth of July and Christmas parties, as well as a few other get-togethers at the common area down by the Sebastian River. Ernie and Lucy Jacoby lived on the next street and I took care of their lawn and later became a "caregiver" to them when their son moved away.

In 1994, after Dad passed away, I continued my visits to Cousin Charles in Palm Coast. As the year wound down and Christmas was approaching, Marian and I were intent on getting the gifts purchased and sent out to the family and friends. I always included in the long list my golfing buddies, golf course attendants, mail and newspaper delivery people, neighbors, my car mechanics, and even the workers at the

New Directions, Opportunities, and Blessings

dump. The list, (which I still have) included more than fifty items. It was fun and all were well-deserved. Restaurant gift cards became a staple of our annual list.

One week before Christmas 1994, I received a phone call that would change my life in many ways. It was Cousin Charles and he sounded desperate over the phone: "Warren I need you. You've got to come and help me!" Thus began a chapter in my life that included lots of travel, health problems of my own, seven years of taking care of all of Charles' needs, and in the end a financial reward that carries us to this very day. After receiving the urgent call, I put all my own plans aside and headed for Palm Coast. When I arrived, I found that Charles had reached the breaking point and a neighbor had called an ambulance to take Charles to the hospital. The neighbor had seen Charles out in the street calling for a wife he did not have! You can imagine what it was like to go to a town I knew nothing about to become the only caregiver and court-appointed guardian. But I did know that "the first thing that I had to do was to get him situated. He was not physically sick and the hospital would not admit him, but it was obvious that he could not go home either. Remembering that it was Christmas week and almost everyone of importance was off or gone away. I was able to have Charles admitted on a very temporary basis to a "respite" part of the hospital where he could stay for only two days. I was in the position of acting as Charles' guardian without any legal basis, so my first item on the agenda was to get in touch with Charles' lawyer. I was fortunate to locate him and get the necessary paperwork done. Then it was back to the hospital to speak to a woman social worker who helped me a great deal and directed me to an assisted living home.

"Concorde Loving Care" was a small home with a capacity of six patients and it was owned and operated by Mrs. Ida Harris, an African

American lady whose father had been a pastor in New York City. Ida was a wonderful lady, kind and caring for all her patients. It was a perfect choice for Charles to spend his remaining seven years. Having him there made it especially easy for me in regard to his care. Once Charles was situated, the New Year would find Marian and me devoting almost full-time to sorting out and organizing his home, belongings, and especially his financial assets.

In order to devote full-time to the legal matters, cleaning his home (which took three full months) and beginning the process of organizing his financial affairs, we often stayed over at the Hampton Inn. Charles had been one of the first residents when Palm Coast was being developed as an ITT company residential community. Nancy Lopez, a famous woman golfer of that period did much of the initial advertising. Charles' house was very modest, as were all of the originals, but it was located on a deep water canal which had access to the Indian River and the Atlantic Ocean. It was interesting to me to see these rather small, modest homes with a huge yacht parked behind them on that canal.

The cleaning began with attempting to tidy up without losing any important checks or legal papers that were anywhere and everywhere. It was not an easy task. We found checks and uncashed money orders, investment information, and other important items in some very unusual places. Then there were the hundreds of bottles of vitamin pills piled up on the dining room table, in every kitchen drawer and cabinet and even in the oven. There were several boxes of unopened vitamins in the front hall where they had been delivered. This company and several others were taking advantage of Charles' inability to keep track of his daily life and affairs.

The initial cleaning was a month-long project and that was just for a starter. We removed thirty large trash bags full of old newspapers and other trash items. Charles had a little red Ford Fiesta which needed to be sold, as did the house and property. A young fellow, Tony, a resident of the neighborhood heard about the car and after taking a test drive, he bought it for $300.00. I had established my legal guardianship with the local bank where I paid many visits. Charles had a Trust account at the First Union Bank and Mr. Mosley was his Trust Officer. His office was in

Daytona Beach. Mr. Schroeder was his CPA who provided information about taxes and other pertinent financial matters. He had handled Charles' account for many years, which proved to be a big asset to me.

Although we were making progress in getting Charles' affairs in order, we could not begin to imagine what was involved. From Christmas week 1994 until even after his death on Feb. 4, 2002, both Marian and I spent many hours each week working on that effort. For me it was often traveling to Palm Coast, Daytona Beach, and other assorted places. The main thing, however, was to visit Charles, personally, at least once a week. My visit included talking with him, which was an adventure in itself. Sometimes he would be very lucid and other times, he would be unable to carry on any kind of conversation, but my visit always included prayer and on his birthday and holidays, we would take a party for the entire facility. Charles had an unusual phobia that was troubling to the Loving Care staff. He was constantly claiming that he hadn't had a bowel movement for months and no matter

Me with Cousin Charles

what actually happened, he insisted. Then one day I had a brainstorm. I purchased a huge calendar and we hung it right over his bed. The caregivers made a big, red mark on the calendar for each "event" and slowly, Charles overcame his fear.

During those seven years, several incidents stand out in my mind, but the "fire" was the greatest. Summers in Florida were always on the hot side, and one particular year it was very hot and exceptionally dry. Brush fires were always a hazard, but in Flagler County, there was one that engulfed the entire area north of Daytona Beach, and Palm Coast was located right in the middle of the danger zone. No warnings had been posted for the Interstate, so I started out on my weekly trek to visit Charles. As I proceeded north on I-95, I could see flames and smoke not far from the highway and a strong wind was blowing. I thought that I'd better get to see Charles and head right home as quickly as possible. So I stopped at Walmart, bought a gift for him, and after a short visit and a prayer, headed south for Sebastian. As I proceeded, it was obvious that the fire was going to cross the Interstate. I was in the southbound lane when I saw the State Troopers setting up roadblocks across in the northbound lanes. As it turned out, I was the last vehicle to get through on the southbound side.

Meanwhile, I heard on the radio that Palm Coast had a mandatory evacuation in place and there was a mad rush of cars heading west on every accessible route. Ida received word that Concorde Loving Care would have to be evacuated and she told the caller that she had no way to evacuate her patients, including Charles, without professional help. The emergency people responded that they would send a bus, which did come. However, in moving the patients who were mostly bedridden, one man had a heart attack and died. As the bus was leaving, the fire was already in the neighborhood and Michelle, Ida's daughter, was to follow in her car with all the medical records and medications and documentation. She loaded her car and tried to follow the bus but found that she had a flat tire. There were lots of firemen nearby and several of them changed the tire, but by that time, the bus with Ida and the patients had disappeared and no one knew what their destination was. It turned out to be a high school auditorium, well to the north of Palm Coast, where cots had been set up on the floor.

For the next three days, I tried to locate Charles, since he was my responsibility and one I truly cared about. I tried the state emergency management, the Salvation Army, and every other source, all to no avail. However, on the third day, I received a call indicating that the entire Loving Care group was safe and would be returning to their own facility.

New Directions, Opportunities, and Blessings

Our life in River's Edge was continuing, too! I was playing golf and fishing as often as possible and Marian was involved with her music activities, women's golf, and bowling with the church group. My other bowling took place at the Ercildune Lanes in Sebastian where I participated with a season-long team. At the end of the season, the league had a special competition night and I was fortunate to roll a game of perfect spares and was rewarded with a cash prize and a special shoulder patch. One of our team members was an older man named "Reb." He had been a member of General Chennault's "Flying Tigers," pilots who had fought in China prior to World War II.

My "All Spares" patch

It was obvious to me on my visits to Charles that his health was failing. Then, on February 4, 2002, I received a call from Ida Harris that he had passed away. I knew that she felt the loss personally; as I did, but both of us could say that we did all we could to make the final years of Charles' life as comfortable as possible. As his life came to an end, a new phase of mine and Marian's began, one that involved the final legal and financial matters. This would take several years and it would greatly affect us personally. Charles' lawyer was brought before the bar on some dealings, disbarred, and replaced by Donald Duncan, who became very important to me. On one of my visits after Charles' death, I asked Mr. Duncan to examine Charles' file. When he did we discovered that in his last dated and signed will, Charles had left his entire estate to me. This made the difference between 40 percent and 100 percent. It was too late to make changes, but I suspected that his former lawyer knew about that will and had deliberately concealed it from me. At any rate, Marian and I still received a substantial amount and we decided to be good stewards of it.

I had had prior dealing with Mark Parsons, a Christian friend who was a broker for Prudential Securities at the time. He later became disillusioned with Prudential and decided to partner with Raymond James Securities as a local agent in Vero Beach, FL, with his own office. I had numerous meetings with Mark shortly after receiving my inheritance and we decided on a mildly conservative, diversified, investment policy.

In addition to investing, we decided to use some cash to upgrade our home. The result was a new roof, a swimming pool, closing in the front to make a screened in porch, extending the back porch to make room for a spa, glassing in a large "Florida" room and many other indoor improvements. What a nice (but modest home we had). We were also able to substantially help Singing Hills, financially. God keeps His wonderful promises and we had kept ours, too. In Malachi 3:10 God promised, "Bring all the tithes into the storehouse that there might be provisions in my house and see if I will not open the windows of heaven and pour out more blessings than you can receive."

Marian and I had experienced numerous physical problems, especially during the stressful time of caring for Charles. Marian had two bouts with cancer, once with breast cancer and the other with bladder cancer. After many visits to the doctors, she won those battles but she also had a persistent lower back problem that required a spinal fusion of the lumbar fifth vertebrae to the sacral first with four screws. Judy came down to Florida and stayed day and night in the hospital with Marian for three days until she was transferred to the rehabilitation hospital for a week in Vero Beach. Judy stayed for two weeks, and was very helpful in keeping the household maintained for both of us. Our solar heated swimming pool and spa had a long and good history of helping both of us with our aches and pains.

As for me, the "Charles care period" had taken its toll and I found myself waking up in the middle of the night with my heart racing and blood pressure rising. One morning we were reading the local paper when I came upon an ad placed by the Sebastian hospital about a sleep clinic there. The ad included a perfect description of the symptoms I was experiencing. I was able to get the necessary doctor's prescription to make an appointment, which required a two-night stay in the hospital facility. On both nights I was attached to many wires like an EKG heart monitor. These were connected to a special computer in another room which monitored my breathing for six hours, both nights. The results showed that I actually stopped breathing more than a hundred times, mostly for just a second or two. But the computer result showed that on one occasion, I stopped for over a minute, much too long. So, in the end I became beneficiary of a CPAP machine and I have worn the mask every night until this very day and have no more sleep apnea.

I also had some worrisome bouts with severe intestinal bleeding and on one Christmas Eve, I wound up in a private room in Sebastian Hospital, awaiting a colonoscopy. Being Christmas, it meant very few staff members on duty. The doctor on call was a Muslim who did not celebrate Christmas and was available to perform the necessary procedure and cauterize the polyp. That night I watched "It's a Wonderful Life," all night as the channel kept rerunning it. But I did get discharged for Christmas the next morning. Dan and Cheri and their son, Nate, came up from Okeechobee and we celebrated the day together. Christmas was always a big thing for us. We decorated extensively, including indoors and out. We had an imitation tree on the front porch, which not only served at Christmas, but Marian decorated it especially for all the holidays, all year long. I hung a giant star on the flagpole which was lighted and highly visible to the neighbors. The trees on either side of the flagpole were lighted with colored lights. Inside our home, there were lights and other Christmas ornaments, always with a Christian emphasis.

One of the most interesting features was my train and village display. It

Our train setup was popular with visitors

started with eight sawhorses as a foundation for the two 4 x 8 foot plywood pieces, making a 4 x 16 foot area. Soon this began to fill up with miniature lighted houses and buildings, a skating rink, carousel, trees, snow, and everything needed to make it special. Various friends and especially our family kept adding features but the highlights for me were the Red Sox train cars, Fenway Park, and other assorted mementos of my favorite team. At every opportunity, we welcomed children, including Marian's piano students to visit our display. Adult visitors enjoyed it, too. Great fun! One of the things we took pleasure in doing was, on special holiday occasions, to invite our neighbors and especially those who would otherwise be alone, to join us around the table for a holiday feast. We appreciated the many times that Cheri came to help with the preparations. We had always felt that one of the gifts of the Spirit is hospitality and there always has been a "Welcome" at our door.

Our years in Florida were punctuated by our annual trips back to Singing Hills. How nice it was to feel we were "home" at both places. The trips, however, provided some exciting side lights. The Melbourne, FL, airport was a new modern facility but was limited by its proximity to Orlando and offered a minimum schedule. On one occasion, however, we were able to book a flight on an Eastern Airlines plane with a stop and connecting flight in Atlanta, GA. The waiting room at Melbourne was at runway level and had a huge window so that we could easily see our plane and what was going on in preparation for the flight. We would be boarding the jet by walking to a portable stair that led to the entrance and seating area. In preparation for the flight, we could see the captain and crew inspecting the plane, and as they did, they discovered that one of the tires was either low on air or entirely flat. That discovery prompted a hasty decision and apparently it was decided to change the wheel and tire. All this was clearly visible to us and our fellow passengers.

Although many of us were especially concerned about missing our connecting flight in Atlanta, the scenario on the tarmac was getting quite humorous. First, the mechanical crew brought in a regular truck jack and attempted to lift the plane to remove the wheel and replace it with another. After much frustration, a much larger lift arrived and the situation was remedied. So we were finally on our way and all of us knew that we would most likely miss our Boston flight. Once in Atlanta, we knew that we would need to hurry, and we were aware from past experiences that the airport had three main concourses. Our Boston flight was scheduled for concourse "B," which required a quick trip on the moving sidewalk and a hasty move to the "B" concourse, Gate 3. I had told Marian to follow, while I rushed, trying to be first in line. However, when I arrived at the gate desk, the attendant said that the plane scheduled for departing was full and already had "standbys" waiting. She checked the computer listings and said that there would be a plane departing for Boston from Gate 31. Since there were many others heading for Boston, the concourse became more like the "Boston Marathon" with all of us scrambling to get to Gate 31 at the far end of the area. I was one of the first to arrive and showed the woman at the arrival desk my tickets which she, for some reason, kept.

In the meantime, Marian arrived and we settled in for a needed rest. Our plane was not yet there; it evidently needed a small repair and was in an area across the huge field. The very nice young woman was doing her best to soothe the passions of the bedraggled group but there was a comforting element, too! The captain and crew were all in the waiting area—so the plane must be going! But our doubts about the flight turned into fears when the crew, except for the pilot, exited the gate area. Since I was never one to exhibit patience in a situation like this, I decided to approach the captain, who was calmly reading the New York Times, and ask about the situation. The news wasn't all that comforting when he said that he and the crew had arrived at this gate well over an hour ago with their 757. They had gone to lunch, come back, and the plane was gone!

Soon after, it became evident that this plane wouldn't be lifting off for Boston and the girl at the desk came on the loud speaker to announce that the flight had been canceled and that there would be another flight available at Gate 5. The Boston Marathon turned into a sprint back down what looked like a raceway. Marian said she would wait at Gate 31 until we had some good news and I took off, running, and arrived in third place at Gate 5, behind two young men. When I got to the desk, the attendant asked for my tickets. "Oh, no!" My tickets were still up at Gate 31, but I asked her to check the computer, which she did and it showed that we had valid tickets but I needed to go back, to get them, and Marian, too. When I got back to the desk, the sympathetic young woman said: "Here are boarding passes for that flight and when they call for passenger boarding, don't say anything; just get in line and find a seat," which we did. It was a smooth flight to Boston but from then on, Atlanta airport was in my vocabulary as the "purgatory" of flying—you could get "in" but there was no way "out." We had many other experiences with our annual flights to and from New Hampshire, but once we got in a groove of flying from Manchester to Orlando on Southwest airlines, scheduled for the same time of day, each time, it actually became a pleasure.

Jayne Bush was always a good sport, whatever happened

On another occasion, Bill and Jayne Bush were traveling back to New Hampshire after sharing a vacation together with us at our Florida home. We made it a "foursome," leaving from Orlando and arriving in Hartford, CT. The flight plan was to embark in Orlando and change planes in Atlanta, (not a good idea). Our flight left Orlando on time but as we proceeded northward, the weather deteriorated with turbulence and soon our pilot was dodging massive thunderstorms which were plainly visible to us, both the clouds and the lightning. We had proceeded to a position about 100 miles from Hartsfield airport when the captain came on to explain that we would need to stay in a flight pattern because a lightning strike had caused damage to a runway at the airport and there was a backup of landing planes. Eventually he came back on to say that we were running low on fuel and that we would be refueling at a field in Montgomery, Alabama, so shortly thereafter, we landed there. The captain said that we could briefly disembark if we wished, so all of the passengers got up and prepared to visit the Montgomery airport which really didn't look too inviting. However, just as we were going to leave, he came back on the loudspeaker to announce that we had been cleared to land in Atlanta and would be taking off immediately. Back into our seats and seat belts and on our way we went. The storms had taken leave, so it was a smooth flight but very late.

Bill Bush was a great musician who often played his saxophone for guests at Singing Hills

We went to an all-too-familiar concourse from which our Hartford flight was to leave, but once again, there was no plane! It was still in Dallas awaiting storms to pass in that area so we settled in with a snack and newspaper until well after midnight when the plane finally arrived for us. After loading the passengers and luggage, we took off and the rest of the flight into Hartford was uneventful. It was almost 2:00 a.m. when we landed. But we were thankful. Bill had left his car at the parking area and we would soon be on our way up Interstate 91. Just to put the final touch to the trip, we found that the car was almost out of gas. Where to go and what to do at 2:30 in the morning to buy gas? We did find a policeman who directed us to an "all night" gas station and we finally arrived back at Singing Hills, just as the first rays of sun were showing in the East. We were tired but happy!

Looking back a few years, one of the most exciting times happened in 2004 when on Labor Day weekend, hurricane Frances was headed directly toward Sebastian. We decided to evacuate our home and head north with a lot of other people. I had called Ida Harris in Palm Coast to see if she could locate a hotel room for us. Her answer was, "No way! You're going to stay with us." On Interstate 95, it was bumper-to-bumper traffic going north at about five miles per hour. After being in that line for more than an hour, we hadn't even reached Titusville and it was then that I had a brainstorm. We should get off at the next exit, find a restaurant with a restroom and head north on U.S. Route 1. This proved to be an excellent decision and except for the traffic lights, it was on to Palm Coast with very little traffic.

After arriving at Ida's, Marian discovered that the nose piece of her eye glasses had broken and they were not wearable. We rushed over to the Walmart store and we were the last ones admitted as the store was closing because of the storm. There was water everywhere. Marian got a quick fix on the glasses and we returned to Ida's to spend that day and night there dealing with the category one storm. The storm had subsided and the sun came out, so for us it would mean an early start back to Sebastian. I envisioned that I-95 would be the same as it had been in the evacuation, with everyone heading home, but when we got to the on-ramp, the highway was almost deserted and we were able to make a fast trip back to Sebastian.

Arriving home, it was great to see that our home had no damage except for the loss of electricity. We were a bit desperate for a cup of coffee so we called our neighbor, Len Brown, to see if he might have some. His answer was, "Sure. Come on over," which we did and had some fresh coffee. But, I wondered why Len's electricity was on and ours was not? Len asked me if I had pulled the master switch back on and I realized, "Oh no, I hadn't." But the best was still to come!

Out in the Caribbean, the atmosphere was coming together to form another ugly lady, "Jeanne." This hurricane was even bigger and become a Category 3 storm with sustained winds of 135 miles per hour and the eye was aiming directly for the Treasure Coast of Florida, right at River's Edge. This time Marian and I decided to ride out the storm at home and trust the Lord for protection. What a night it was! Our weather radio kept coming on with warnings to go to a safe room. In our case it would be in the hallway between the two bedrooms and the bath, a small area with many partitions. However, we opted for couches in the middle of the house but found it hard to get any sleep. At the height of the storm, the roar of the wind, the rain beating on the shuttered windows and branches landing on the roof, made it sound like we were in a battle. The storm passed and in the morning a few welcome rays of sun showed through the small openings in the hurricane shutters.

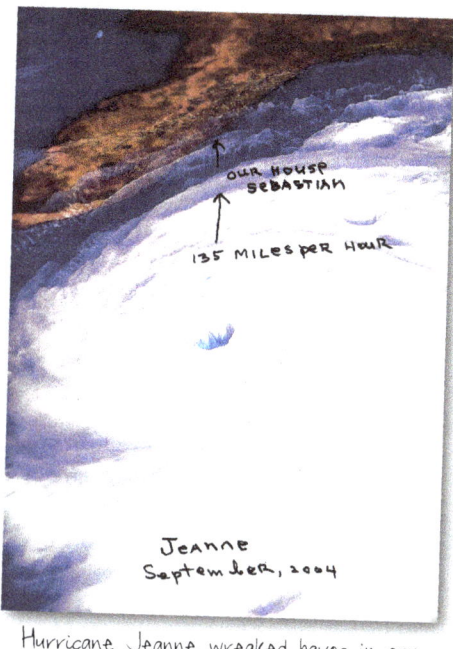

Hurricane Jeanne wreaked havoc in our region of the "Treasure Coast."

The wind had subsided and "Jeanne" was gone but what a mess she left behind! My first job was to evaluate the damage to our home and property. After removing the corrugated aluminum hurricane shutters from all the doors and windows, I walked around the outside with my video camera and was grateful to find that our house had not sustained any roof or structural damage. Five screen panels surrounding our enclosed pool had been blown out and a big pine tree had bent over (very unusual) and taken out the windshield of my boat. It had also fallen on our small porch extension which covered our spa and collapsed the aluminum roof. These relatively small damages would need to be repaired and the huge tree with many limbs removed. Dan and Cheri arrived on the scene soon after and did a great job of going to work on the fallen tree, removing the branches to the street in front of the house to form a huge pile. Later some truckers from Georgia removed the pile to the fairgrounds, which became totally littered with branches and logs retrieved from the entire county.

After checking our own home, I took the camera for a tour of River's Edge. What I found wasn't pretty! Most of the forty-nine homes had sustained damage to their roofs and those that bordered the river had interior damage from the water. In some, a mixture of water and mud had flooded the kitchen cabinetry, walls and flooring, making the house unlivable. Florida became known as the "blue tarp" state because so many damaged roof tops were temporarily protected with blue tarps. The next consideration for us was power and fortunately I had a gasoline powered generator. We were able to bring sandwiches and coffee and TV dinners to our neighbors that day and Publix supermarket had laid in a large shipment of five-pound ice bags. On the adjacent street to ours, "walking catfish" had followed the flood waters onto land and were flopping around on the pavement as the water receded. Sebastian, itself, had taken a very big hit! Besides the 135 mile-per-hour sustained wind, the storm had spawned small tornadoes which seemed to pick out a specific house or tree area to strike. Some of our friends lost their roof while the next door neighbors had no damage at all. There was one two-story home on Main Street that had the whole second floor blown off. The small low house in between the two larger ones sustained no damage; the second floor of the first house was carried right over the lower one. Along the river and especially on the ocean shore, many homes were completely destroyed, and highway Route One was undermined and partially washed away. What an experience this was and how thankful we were that the Lord had spared us, but we did what we could to help others, especially in our neighborhood. The toll was great, but things were beginning to recover. Barefoot Bay, a large community of manufactured homes, was almost totally destroyed and many of the homes had to be replaced. So it was that Marian and I had experienced two major hurricanes, just two weeks apart and we were, personally, no worse for the wear! Thank you, Lord!

New Directions, Opportunities, and Blessings   189

Although we were still sharing our year between Sebastian and Singing Hills, the time frame was gradually changing toward a longer stay at 7 Gail Road. Dave and Ilona had moved to Sebastian, not far from us. That property extended down to the shore of the Sebastian River where it was easy to cast your line from a comfortable chair. The bonus was that the river was home to a good variety of fish, large and small. At times you could find a school of small red snappers and at other times, some large sharks. Dave caught a thirty-five pound black tip shark one night from the shore. It took forty-five minutes of fighting to land it. I was the "net man" in this case, and the shark was so large its head barely fit into the net. It was exciting, too, to see the manatees, especially in the winter months. They were seeking the warmer water of the river and sometimes came right up to the edge of the bank to munch on water plants. What a beautiful setting it was, one that inspired many pictures. One photo shows a cloud in the shape of an eagle, or perhaps an angel. Dave made it into a poster and also used it as a cover for one of the authors of his publishing endeavor.

This looked like an angel or an eagle to Dave and me as the sun went down

Our 80th Birthday celebrations, mine in 2008 and Marian's in 2009, were family sharing times that we deeply appreciated and will never forget. So much time and energy was invested in planning these events to make every detail special! Each "party" was uniquely designed around our individual interests and yet there was the common theme through it all—love, the Lord's love for us and our love for one another. My 60 years' of cheering on the Red Sox was the theme of the family picnic-party. From the shirts to the hats to the hot dogs to the special cake to EVERYTHING Bosox, it was fabulous. Just look at that table top. Later that day, we enjoyed a family hymn sing that made me think I was in heaven. You know the lyrics, "Daddy sang bass, Momma sang tenor. . . ." Well, it was almost like that except I can't carry a tune in a bucket, so to speak, so I took the photo.

Marian's celebration was a lot lower key, at her request. Yet all the special attention to detail that had been invested in my honor a year earlier also marked her "party." There was a special cake, and some special gifts, and dinner for all at the Lobster Shanty in Vero Beach. There was also a special song in church, performed by eight family members, Marian's favorite: "The Longer I Serve Him, the Sweeter He Grows." And then there were the "Voice Quilts" for each of us, which are high tech and beautifully crafted "Music Boxes." You open the cover, and you hear your friends, new and old, and from far and near, who have recorded their personal greetings and reminiscences for your special day. Such a wonderful and meaningful and thoughtful nostalgia smorgasbord!

As time went by I worked diligently on our yard and added a variety of plants and trained a huge hedge that extended all the way around the rear and side yards. We called it our "Christmas hedge" because it blossomed into a carpet of red blossoms just before Christmas and continued until late March. Our bird feeders attracted a great variety of birds but our favorites were families of painted buntings and occasional

New Directions, Opportunities, and Blessings

My 80th birthday Red Sox—themed family lunch — wow!

Even at Marian's 80th birthday party I got to open presents!

My Voice Quilt — what a special gift!

Marian's 80th Birthday celebration was great fun, too!

Our family hymn sing was one highlight of a wonderful day

humming birds. The Christmas hedge was fast growing and provided a nice privacy fence, but it needed trimming often to keep it under control so I could reach the top in order to trim it. It required 150 feet of trimming on both sides. I believe it was a variety of honeysuckle. I started with a gas trimmer, but as the years went by, I switched to electric because of the weight of the machine. In the end, the yard and its care was a contributing factor to help persuade us that we should begin to think about our future.

In 2010, Dave encouraged me to finish a book that I had started several years earlier called *The Other Side of Life*, and he published it for me. Actually, it was the first of three books. I thank him for inspiring me to begin writing again. The second book, called *The Big Black Book* was also one that I had written earlier. Mrs. Alyce Spinosa, a good friend and member of the Forest Park Baptist Church did some wonderful illustrating for the book, including animals, trees, and people. 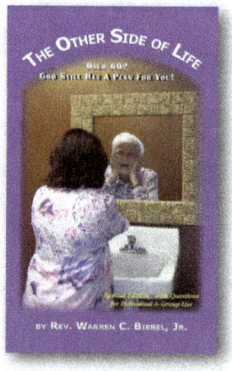 Alyce was a small wiry type of woman and had accompanied us on trips to Fort Lauderdale for the Christmas Pageant at First Baptist church, there. Her husband, Al sat next to me on the trips and told stories about his time as a detective in New York City. After Al died, Alyce continued on as President of her condominium association. A wonderful woman!

Through the years of my ministry, I had always used the King James Version of the Bible. In fact, I had memorized large portions, especially of the New Testament, including almost the entire book of Romans. I loved the beautiful flowing language and found that somehow it was easier to memorize than more modern versions. However, I realized

New Directions, Opportunities, and Blessings

that many young people just weren't getting it, so I believe the Lord led me to write the book *We've Got Mail*, my own paraphrase of the New Testament letters. The beautiful cover was done by Adrian Vergin, Ilona's son, and once again it was Dave who kept me moving on the book. It was completed and published in 2009, 2010, and 2011. I thank you, Lord for such a great privilege.

Neighbors

Marian and I had been caregivers for my Mom and Dad and I had continued that job for the seven years with Charles. After a brief respite, I became a part-time caregiver for an elderly couple in our neighborhood in River's Edge—Ernie and Lucy Jacoby. I had begun by taking care of their lawn and property. Their son, who had lived nearby, had moved to Michigan and they were left alone. At first they were able to manage their home and affairs, but as time went on they needed more assistance. Marian and I would take them out to dinner or a picnic by

Ernie and Lucy Jacoby were our neighbors in River's Edge

the river, often. At Christmas, I would climb up a "pull down" ladder in the garage and bring down a whole array of ornaments and a well-worn tree. I would set it up for them and trim the upper part. As the years passed, I gradually realized that part of my life's calling was to be an "encourager" to my family, friends, and neighbors. It is a continuing part of my life now, as well as Marian's.

After worshiping for seventeen years at Forest Park Baptist Church in Vero Beach, we decided that it was time for us to be closer to our home in Sebastian and we chose the Sebastian River Baptist Church. While at Forest Park we had done just about everything. I had preached, served on boards and, most importantly, presided over the sale of our old church building, downtown, which had been severely damaged by the hurricane and was badly in need of repairs. The congregation was able to purchase another church building, in pristine condition, from a church that was relocating and building a new building. We were able to negotiate a settlement that allowed our congregation to realize two million dollars to invest for the future, as well as having a newer and more modern building in a nicer neighborhood location.

Jack & Louise Rafferty

Marian had been active in providing piano music and organizing the choir. We also organized group trips, including mission's trips all the way to Singing Hills in New Hampshire. Leaving some of our longtime friends in the church was a tough decision but we continued luncheon dates; especially with Jack and Louise Rafferty.

Meanwhile, it wasn't long at Sebastian River Baptist that we were again immersed in the ministry. Marian was working with the choir and preparing special programs for Christmas and Easter. I was preaching once a month on Sunday evenings. Our pastor was a former marine who worked full-time for a huge citrus company where he was in charge of maintenance. He was not seminary trained but had a very good knowledge of the Bible and was really an evangelist at heart. One

New Directions, Opportunities, and Blessings

couple, who found the Lord there, was Herb and Isabel Buscher, who became good friends of ours. They made unique custom-made marine furniture in Miami. They were a breath of fresh air to the church with their enthusiasm when they were converted and baptized. We found that we had a lot in common with them and visited together frequently. As was mentioned earlier, Isabel spearheaded the yard sale we had before moving and bought a lot of the collectible items for her children, plus anything nautical.

Herb and Isabel Buscher

Our church was located on Route One, which followed the Indian River along the coast of Florida. That made it especially vulnerable to storms that came in off the ocean. One evening, during the evening service, there was a loud bang, the lights went out and a small fire started in the fuse box near the entrance. A small tornado had blown through and wiped out one of the main transformers on the telephone pole just outside the church entrance. Another memorable event happened when the Pastor became ill during his sermon and hurriedly asked me to take over. I had made a decision early on, never to say no to an opportunity to serve, so I gladly stepped in to finish the service. So it was that we completed our worship experience in Florida there and when it came time to say goodbye, we received a beautiful plaque, thanking us for our service.

Our "Thank You" plaque from Sebastian River Baptist Church

Saving the Best for Last

—m—

Back Home in New Hampshire

SOMETIME IN 2010, Don and Judy had come for a vacation visit and they floated the first idea about us coming back to New Hampshire to live with them. This would require building a new home and living together, in separate apartments, while sharing the kitchen. It would mean a sacrifice for them and a wonderful solution for us.

The Cornish, NH—Windsor, VT Covered Bridge

  Dan was facing retirement from teaching, and he and Cheri had decided to move back to Wyoming to be near their children and grandchildren. Dave and Ilona had moved away from our area to Orlando and were "itching" to get back to Colorado, as soon as it could work out for them. We had been having some physical challenges so this seemed like the obvious choice. So, Don, Judy, and Paul began work on plans for a new, custom built, geothermal home on property that Don

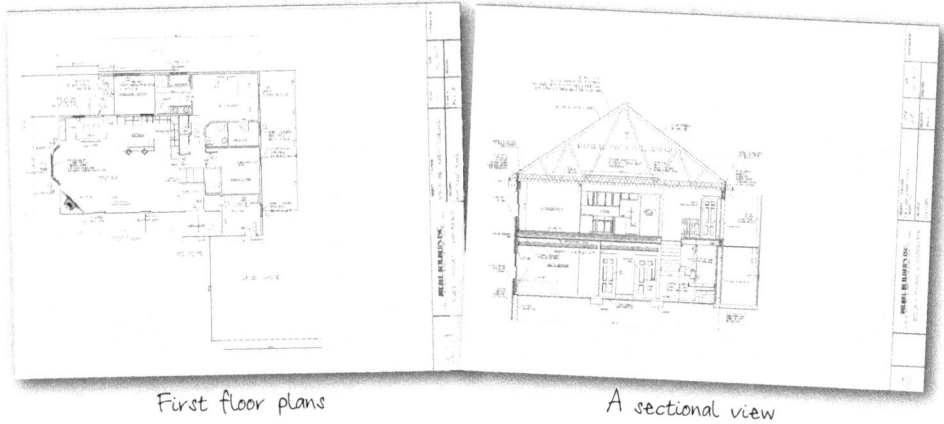

First floor plans A sectional view

had inherited from his parents. It was exciting for us to see the pictures, as they developed, of the proposed location and building. There have been a number of life-changing decisions that we have made along the way but in this case, it would take a miracle to complete all the logistics, not just for us, but for Judy and Don.

Among the specific challenges was the design of the new house and that project fell to Paul, Don, and Judy. On our end, the number one matter was the sale of our house at a price that would contribute enough toward the construction of the new one. We discussed this in a preliminary way with a real estate agent whom we knew well. Her estimate of what our home might bring was disappointing. We also had to give serious thought to which of our furniture and heirlooms could go with us and if and how they would fit into the new house, sight unseen. It was with great reluctance that we decided that most of our "stuff" would have to go. The list we prepared started with items that we would definitely like to keep.

Then there were other things, including most of my train and village display along with Marian's doll collection that would have to go. Twenty years of living had produced a wide variety of pictures, trinkets, and the like. Also, there were lots of tools and some machines. The result was a huge yard sale which was very successful. We had help arranging and selling the items with family and friends, especially Dan, Cheri, and our friend Isabel, who was the best customer for the dolls

Saving the Best for Last – Back Home in New Hampshire

and village houses, and so forth for the train layout. Some other friends from the church were also a great help. We gave Herb and Isabel some of our Florida Ocean and boat pictures which fit in with their home décor. In the end, almost all the items in the yard sale were sold and the rest went to the thrift shop the very same day, thanks to Cheri.

The real estate estimate had been $100,000 realized after expenses, but we felt that our house was worth much more than that and had decided to part with all the furnishings except our bed and some other items. The furnishings would be included in the sale.

In the meantime, progress was moving forward in New Hampshire, with land being surveyed, septic requirements met, the design fine-tuned and actual excavation and grounds preparation begun. In Florida, we had taken a sizeable loan against our assets with Raymond James Bank to help with construction. It was decided that this house would consist of two stories. We would have an apartment on the upstairs ground floor level and Don and Judy's full-size apartment would be on the lower floor with a walk-out door, also on ground level since the construction is on a hillside. We would share the kitchen and have meals together most of the time. The "Great Room" was an inspiration to enjoy with great views and lots of space for some of our old furniture, as well as the new.

Our finished home with solar panel array

One of the most important features of the home was that it was solar powered and geothermal, with thirty-nine solar panels and a heat producing system that uses water from our 400 foot artesian well, by compression, to produce heat. An inspection by a State agency awarded our home a five-star plus rating, one of the best in the state.

Matters in Florida had not yet been settled. We hadn't proceeded with the real estate company or advertised widely. Could we sell the house at the price we needed? The answer came, unexpectedly, one evening when the doorbell rang and our neighbors, John and Susan Coard, entered to announce that they wanted to buy our house at the asking price of $140,000.00, which also included some very nice furniture. This was a special answer to prayer!

John and Susan wanted our home so that they could move her parents from Maryland to be near to them. This would be a perfect solution for them and for us. There was no need for an agent's fee and we settled directly with the Paradise Title Company, in Indian River County.

Now we needed to arrange the actual logistics of moving. We settled on a sixteen foot rental truck which Dan and Cheri graciously offered to drive to New Hampshire. It would also tow a trailer carrying our Toyota Rav4. Dan and a friend, Tim, came to help move the heavier items into the truck. We were especially grateful for all the help in the whole operation. Special thanks to Dan, Cheri, Dan's friend, Tim, Dave and Ilona who did the final closing up of the house, and several other friends who helped! The Florida phase of our move would soon end, so we said goodbye to our neighborhood and church friends. We had experienced a wonderful twenty-one year interlude in our lives and throughout those years, the Lord allowed us to serve Him and be good friends and witnesses to hundreds of people.

We took what probably would be our last flight from Orlando, FL, on Southwest airlines to Manchester, NH, on March 23, 2013. Don and Judy met us. We were back home in New Hampshire to celebrate our 64th wedding anniversary eight days later. Since construction on the new house wasn't complete, Dan and Cheri's long drive with the truck ended at our original house, at Singing Hills, which was still at that time Don and Judy's home. This necessitated unloading and storing the many household and personal items that filled the rental truck to capacity. Somehow, space was found in the old office and other areas of the downstairs. It was like a big puzzle trying to find certain items that we needed before we could unpack everything. Judy accommodated us with a bedroom and another room to set up as an office, with an extra bureau and another closet and storage space. We were to be there for six months.

While waiting for the house to be completed there was plenty to do. We had a very pleasant surprise when we took our Toyota Rav4 to Howe Motors to make a trade. Ed Malhoit, the salesman, suggested that we lease a brand new Rav4, AWD, with features like a back-up camera, for three years, at no cost after the trade and free maintenance for 20,000 miles or two years. Actually we received a surprise check for over $3,000.00 from Toyota Company for the additional value of the vehicle we traded in. Once again, Marian and I were thanking the Lord for His wonderful provision. There were plenty of legal and financial arrangements that we needed to make. These included New Hampshire driver licenses, car registrations, banking arrangements, local voter registration, and meeting with our attorney, who is also our friend. As I write now, my memories of this entire venture merge into a sort of vivid dream. Could we really have made all these moves and decisions in our early 80s? The answer is no, not without God's wisdom and our family's encouragement and assistance.

Speaking of dreams, my dream of a gazebo for Singing Hills became a reality when we purchased a beautiful gazebo and it was delivered and set up on a nice location overlooking the valley, on August 10, 2014. It was my vision that individuals, families, and small groups could gather there for special moments of quiet worship and fellowship.

The gazebo had been a dream of mine for years

Our beautiful new energy-efficient home was fast taking shape and Judy was immersed in painting the inside. That was a really hard job that took a couple of months but saved lots of money. At the same time the landscaping was going forward with a huge blower mounted on a truck with a hopper where seed and mulch were loaded simultaneously and then shot out over the almost three acres of yard surface. This would later become a beautiful lawn. As this was going forward and the driveway was complete, I purchased thirteen young blue spruce trees and planted them along the drive, spaced twenty feet apart. Among other trees that we planted in a separate area, hoping for a small future orchard, were apple and pears and close to the house other trees and bushes were also planted.

Saving the Best for Last – Back Home in New Hampshire

One special tree was a red oak, planted in memory of the four family children who left us to be with the Lord. As that tree grows to be fifty feet high, my prayer is that these precious ones will never be forgotten. An American flag is displayed too, on the hill just above the Red Oak. Later, in the spring of 2014, we added an equipment shed to house our small landscaping machines and tools. During our first winter, the snow blower had blown gravel out onto the lawn and so on October 8, 2014, we had the driveway paved. This proved to be a great move on our part, because the winter of 2014-2015 provided a real test for our home. Starting with Thanksgiving, a blanket of white surrounded us and below zero temperatures became the norm for February. Our home passed the test with flying colors and then in March we received our first seed and flower catalog and if we daydreamed hard enough we could envision beautiful flowers and green grass!

Even in the winter, our nearly net zero home kept us toasty warm

Now as we complete this book, that grass is like a green carpet around our place here in Plainfield, NH; the orchard has produced a little fruit, and there seem to be flowers everywhere. Isn't that what heaven is like, as described in God's Word? Our home and setting here are beautiful, but we know that Jesus has "prepared a place" for us that will be so much better.

Well, my life began on May 18, 1928 and God has another date in mind for me in the not too distant future. But if you have read this book the way I hoped you would, you will know that for me, it has been, and will continue to be, a journey with Him.

THE MIRROR OF MY LIFE

In the chambers of my imagery, I saw myself
Young and full of hope!
Later, I saw myself, indulged in life,
So busy—so many plans.
Then I saw another person—real!
And I knew that time was fleeing away.
Then I saw the Lord, caring and loving.
I knew He still had a plan for me.
Then I understood the really important
Things in life
These were already mine! And so . . .
I no longer needed to dream a dream of life
Because God's kind of life belongs to me!

~ WCB

Country life allows us to continue the journey together

Photographs

THE LAST PART OF THIS BOOK IS A "PHOTO ALBUM" OF MY LIFE, IN three sections:

Our Family Through the Years

Singing Hills Friends & Projects

To Love and to Cherish. . . .

Please note that the selection of these photos, or the inclusion of any other photos in this book involved difficult choices including space limits and so forth.

Knowing that we simply could not include every photo of the literally thousands that we have in our possession meant that some that we might wish to have included had to be left out.

This should not be taken by anyone left out to mean that the intersection of your life with ours was less important than those that are shown. In fact, the primary message of all that I've written and all the photos that we have been able to include is that I am deeply gratitude for the constructive roles that the Lord allowed us to have in each other's lives, for that is His way . . . to use simple folks like us to make a significant difference in the lives of others, and therefore, for His good purpose in our world.

In gratitude to Him, and to you all,

~WCB

Our Family Through the Years

**Herman Biebel about 1902
Driver-Steamer Eng. Co. #6
Bridgeport Fire Department**

My grandfather, Herman Biebel,
with horse drawn fire wagon

My Mother at age three

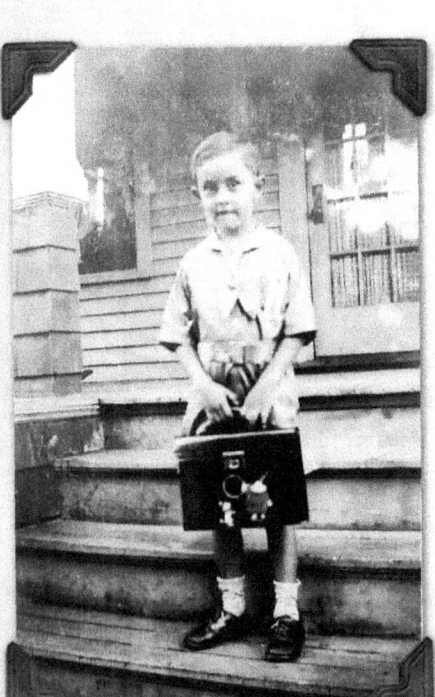

This is how I looked on my
first day of school

My Parents in earlier and happier times

I always enjoyed spending time with my cousins

This is one family gathering at the cottage on Lordship Beach.
How did everyone fit in?

Dave is wondering what kind of a pony this is

Hunting was a family experience

Our four children, circa 1959

(L to R) Dave, Dan, Paul & Judy

The boys and I spent a lot of time boating & fishing

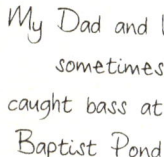

My Dad and I sometimes caught bass at Baptist Pond

Dave convinced my father and Marian's to sit on Paul's motorcycle

This is our family in October 1978

Our kids again, in 2008 — (L to R) Dan, Dave, Paul, & Judy

Our family gathered for our 60th Anniversary in 2009

The ladies went shopping; the boys, golfing.

Marian with great-grandchildren Madison and Kellen Surrette, 2013

Marian with Jack Jones, one of her 17 living great-grandchildren

Don and me at a Red Sox game — Red Sox fans are tough!

My Tribute to Bill and Alice Jordan

It is an honor to offer a heartfelt tribute to Bill and Alice Jordan (the parents of our son-in-law, Don Jordan) who were everyday folks, the kind that everyone would treasure as close friends. As we were getting Singing Hills started, they saw the vision and were two very important people in the process. They did everything from working in the kitchen, as well as cleaning and maintaining, indoors and out. They probably volunteered more hours than they were paid for.

After Bill recovered from his heart transplant, he was right there with me again as we prepared, planted, and cared for massive lawns and fields. His prior farming knowledge and experience were most helpful. It was unique that Don became Director of Singing Hills and had to oversee his father, mother, father-in-law, mother-in-law, and wife. We all worked in unison with many varied responsibilities and really liked each other. We shared our children, grandchildren, and great-grandchildren. Their most important contribution to Marian and me is that they gave us a great son-in-law; now we share our home with him on what was formerly their property, overlooking the old family farmhouse that was built in 1764. Our memories are all pleasant, both with working together and fellowshipping at other times, whether in Florida or in New Hampshire.

Singing Hills

~

Friends

and

Projects

Earl King was always involved, shown here preparing ground for the lodge foundation

The main lodge was built from lumber cut and milled on site

Horace Evans kept the wood fires burning in exchange for a room

So much brush, so little time

Sometimes things seemed just too big to tackle, but eventually we won

Snowblowing with the Kubota kept me busy in winter

Original Chapel & Family Center Design

It took the support of many special friends to fund the chapel & family center

The main chapel took some serious crane work

Son Dan and Grandson Nate, with stonewall they built

Brig & Chris Judy became missionaries to North American Indians as a result of our youth ministry

Birdie and Bob Corbitt. Birdie's water colors beautified the lodge's interior

George & Betty Chapin gave a day a week doing errands for Singing Hills

Dave & Ruth Finlaw spent an entire summer volunteering in various ways

Two pair of Browns — Robin & Ron, in back; Chip & Marian Brown in front — all great friends and supporters

The second wing of the Family Center was not in the original plan, but it was always in my mind

This was one of our first Golf Gathering Groups

Ed & Elsa Tierney from Claremont, whose support never waned

Marian & Earl King, in a more formal moment

We named our second chapel in honor of the Kings

Son Dan nearly single-handedly cleared and then replanted the camping area, with pavilion in background

Our lifelong friends, with me and Marian — Flo and Cecil Breton

The main lodge with Family Center behind

To Love

and

To Cherish . . . .

March 31, 1949

A kiss is still a kiss

We had lots of fun in this boat

Marian joined me on board from time to time

September 2015

Christmas 2015

We really enjoyed our new home in NH

www.ingramcontent.com/pod-product-compliance
Lightning Source LLC
Chambersburg PA
CBHW071606080526
44588CB00010B/1044